A CALL
to
CONSECRATION

Ray Llarena

A Call to Consecration
Copyright © 2024 by Ray Llarena

Published by:

McDougal Publishing
P.O. Box 3595
Hagerstown, MD 21742-3595

ISBN 978-1-581581-212-3
eBook: 978-1-58158-216-1

Printed on demand in the US, the UK, and Australia
For Worldwide Distribution

DEDICATION

To all those who desire more of God. When we give more of ourselves to Him, He gives more of Himself to us.

For Moses had said, **Consecrate yourselves today to the Lord**, even every man upon his son, and upon his brother; that he may bestow upon you a blessing this day.

—Exodus 32:29

Other Books by Ray Llarena

Founded on the Rock   ISBN 978-1-884369-91-9

In Search of Significance   ISBN 978-1-884369-67-4

En busca de proposito   ISBN 978-1-58158-204-8

God's Vision, Our Mission   ISBN 978-1-58158-210-7

Look What the Lord Has Done ISBN 978-1-58158-209-3

CONTENTS

FOREWORD BY HAROLD MCDOUGAL

How do you turn around an ailing church? How do you inspire people who have grown tired of the failures of men and are discouraged by the lack of vision on the part of their leadership? How do you challenge people to pay back huge sums of money that were either misappropriated or stolen by others? How do you challenge people who have lost their missionary vision?

When Bishop Ray Llarena took over the ailing Faith Tabernacle in downtown Chicago many years ago, he faced all of these problems and more. He knew that only God could turn such a situation around, so rather than dwell on the problems of the past, he challenged the people to draw near to God, giving themselves afresh and anew in consecration and dedication to His plan for them as individuals and for the church.

In a few short years, he was able to turn the church around. It became a thriving congregation of many thousands making an impact on the community and on the world. It had paid off its massive debt, totally remodeled its facilities, and was now in a position to make a difference in outreaches and missions locally and around the globe.

How did Pastor Ray do this? He did it using teachings like the ones contained in the pages of this book. These teachings will work for any church in any time period. They are as fresh and vital today as ever. Consider them your personal call to action. Be blessed as you read *A Call to Consecration.*

Harold McDougal

CHAPTER 1

A CALL TO CONSECRATION: PART I

Give, and it shall be given unto you; good measure, pressed down, and shaken together, and running over, shall men give into your bosom. For with the same measure that ye mete withal it shall be measured to you again. Luke 6:38

I want to issue a call to consecration. Beloved, we need to be consecrated to the Lord, and we need to live a life that is consecrated to God. What does *consecration* mean? The words *consecration, dedication, gratefulness,* and *surrender* are very important in the life of any believer. The measure of your receiving from God will be determined by the measure of how much you give of yourself to Him.

In business, the return on your investment depends on how much you have invested. When your capital investment is large, the return can also be large. Of course, if there are problems in the business world, there could be a loss, and the loss could also be great. But a good businessman never focuses on his loses; he concentrates more on his potential gains. The more money you put into a business, the more possibility of prosperity, progress, and increase you will have.

It is the same with our Christian lives. The more we invest of our life, our energy, and our time in the things of God, in the work of God, in spiritual things, supernatural things, the more we can expect to receive in return.

The Scriptures tells us that God returns our investment *"pressed down, shaken together, and running over."* That's His promise.

Giving to God involves a lot more than money. We have received many teachings on the money aspect of our investment, but not nearly enough teaching on investing our time, our energy, our abilities, and our influence—everything we have and everything we are. When we surrender all to God, dedicating all that we are and all that we have, the possibility of the return is immeasurable. You cannot imagine what God will do through you and for you. How does one measure the power and the anointing of God that will move and flow through you to accomplish what

A Call to Consecration

God has determined in His heart and in His mind to carry out through you?

Think about it. God is calling us to consecration. This is a call for every believer, from church pastors down to the humblest member of a congregation. It is to the rich and to the poor among us alike. God is calling.

Our generation needs to hear the Gospel. Therefore, God is calling us all to a life of consecration, a life of dedication, a life of commitment. These are all attributes that are lacking in our Christian world today. We need more commitment, dedication, consecration, faithfulness, stability, and endurance in the Lord.

That these are lacking is a tragedy, for it is these elements that can make us great in the sight of the Lord. These attributes can open doors to God's divine revelation of truth. When this truth is imparted to us, we can experience the fullness of the power of God as He desires to reveal it.

For Moses had said, Consecrate yourselves today to the LORD, even every man upon his son, and upon his brother; that he may bestow upon you a blessing this day.   Exodus 32:29

To whom are we to consecrate ourselves? To the Lord. When are we to consecrate ourselves to the Lord? Today. What does such a consecration involve? It involves giving your life to the Lord, being faithful to the Lord, being committed to the Lord.

Moses was addressing the children of Israel. He first mentioned to them the consecration required, and then he laid out the return: *"that he may bestow upon you a blessing this day."* There was to be a blessing, a return on the investment. This offered gain, of course, was what got the people's attention. Human nature wants to know the return. We are unwilling to invest in something that offers no return.

When someone seems "too nice" to us, we begin to wonder what they might have up their sleeve. They seem to be up to something. They must want something from us. But God isn't joking, and He has nothing to hide. He is ready to bless us if and when we are ready to consecrate our lives to Him. When we respond to the call of consecration, we're opening the windows of Heaven, and blessings will come pouring out. That is the promise of the Word of God.

A Call to Consecration

Again, when was this consecration to be made? Today. And when was the promised blessing to come forth? Tomorrow? Next week? Next month? Next year? No, *"this day"* — today. If you consecrate your life to God today, God will bestow upon you a blessing today. So, don't wait for tomorrow.

> *The gold for things of gold, and the silver for things of silver, and for all manner of work to be made by the hands of artificers. And who then is willing to consecrate his service this day unto the* LORD?   1 Chronicles 29:5

This was David speaking, and he was talking about the Temple his son, Solomon, was building for God in Jerusalem. It was to be made of the best and most costly materials, and those materials were to be donated by God's people. David had already gathered many materials, but there was room for further donations.

These most costly materials were to be handled by the very best artisans available. For the most part, God had already named them, but there was room for other helpers as well. David asked, *"Who is willing to consecrate his service today unto the* LORD?" This shows us that consecration to God is never by force. It is a decision each of us must make.

God is not demanding our consecration; He is giving us an invitation to consecration. This is not to be a consecration at gunpoint. "Do this, or I'll blow your head off!" Consecration to God must be done willingly, voluntarily, not by force, not by demand, not by constraint.

Anything that we do willingly we can do joyfully, and anything that you do joyfully is something you enjoy. When you are forced to do something, you might do it, but it will be with much grumbling and unhappiness. Being forced to do something is never enjoyable, and if we were to make a consecration to God by force, we could not expect to receive the promised reward. This consecration, this dedication, this life of faithfulness to God must be done willingly.

When we do something willingly, it is because we have determined to do it. We have decided in our own heart that we want to do it. Therefore, we have purposed in our heart that we will carry out what we have decided to do from the willingness of our heart. When the heart is willing, it works. As the old saying goes, "Where there's a will, there's a way."

A Call to Consecration

The reason that many twenty-first century Christians are lukewarm in their worship and service to God is that they have not willed in their heart to serve Him with everything they have. When you are fully committed to God, there is nothing you can't accomplish, as hard as it might seem.

When your heart is willing, serving God becomes effortless. When you heart is not willing, everything becomes burdensome and difficult.

Isaiah declared:

If ye be willing and obedient, ye shall eat the good of the land. Isaiah 1:19

You will partake of the goodness of God, eat of the blessings of God, and receive the reward of God if you are willing and if you are obedient. No wonder Jesus prayed that most powerful of all prayers in the Garden of Gethsemane:

And he went a little farther, and fell on his face, and prayed, saying, O my Father, if it be possible, let this cup pass from me: nevertheless not as I will, but as thou wilt. Matthew 26:39

17

What was Jesus saying? He was saying, "Father, if it be possible, let Calvary pass Me by. Let the cross pass Me by. Let the agony of the sacrifice to be made here pass Me by. Let this most painful suffering pass Me by." But then, He realized, this was to say: "Let Your plan of salvation pass Me by. Let Your eternal purposes for all mankind pass Me by." And this compelled Him to add, *"Nevertheless, not as I will* [not My desire, not what I want], *but as thou wilt."*

The reason salvation is ours today, the reason we are enjoying the blessing of God, the reason we have freedom in the Holy Ghost, the reason we are experiencing a supernatural move of God is because Jesus Christ was willing to consecrate His life to the purposes of God, to the plan of God, even if it caused Him suffering and death.

A divided heart is an unfaithful heart, and the heart of far too many Christians is divided, and the consequence is that they are unfaithful to the Lord and His work. God is asking us to be willing. Paul wrote:

For the love of Christ constraineth us.
                              2 Corinthians 5:14

A Call to Consecration

What did he mean by that? He meant that God's love is the force that moves us. The love of Christ is the thing that cultivates the desire to worship and serve Him. His love motivates and challenges us to consecrate our lives to eternal things.

The wise King Solomon wrote:

My son, give me thine heart, and let thine eyes observe my ways.   Proverbs 23:26

Solomon's desire was that his children would consecrate themselves to God and follow His ways. There is a desire in the heart of every man, woman, boy, and girl to serve the Creator, but unless we give our heart to God, that desire will never be realized. Desire is not enough. Plans are not enough. They may be very good plans, but that's not enough. Plans, ideas, desires, and imaginations are all wonderful, but if we don't do something about them, they will just remain plans. A plan that is not carried out is useless and empty.

God is saying, "My son, my child, my daughter, give Me your heart." When you give your heart to God, you will be able to consecrate yourself to Him. Jesus said:

*Out of the abundance of the heart the mouth spea-
keth.* Matthew 12:34

Moses prepared the people:

*And thou shalt love the LORD thy God with all
thine heart, and with all thy soul, and with all thy
might.* Deuteronomy 6:5

*And now, Israel, what doth the LORD thy God
require of thee, but to fear the LORD thy God, to
walk in all his ways, and to love him, and to serve
the Lord thy God with all thy heart and with all
thy soul.* Deuteronomy 10:12

We are to love God, not just with a portion of our
heart, not just part of our heart, not one-tenth of our
heart, not even ninety percent of our heart, but with
all our heart, the totality of our being.

Everything we do proceeds from the heart, even
though it is first manufactured in the mind. It's
almost like an assembly line. It's conceived in the
mind. Then it goes down the conveyor belt to the
heart. When it leaves the heart, that's when action
takes place.

A Call to Consecration

When speaking of the heart, your emotions are involved, your desires are involved, and your feelings are involved. "Give me your heart," God is saying, "not just your riches, your intellect, or your position in life. Nothing else but your heart will do." If God has control of your heart, He can control everything about you.

There's a song that says:

In our hearts, we're undivided
Worshiping one Savior, one Lord
In our hearts, we're undivided
Bound by His spirit forevermore
Undivided[1]

Nothing can divide us when our hearts are knit together, consecrated together for the purpose of God. We can face any obstacle. We can carry any burden, and we'll be able to fulfill our mission because our hearts are united, given to God completely His purposes. *"My son, give me thine heart."*

Paul wrote to his spiritual son Timothy:

1. Songwriters: Bon Jovi, Falcon, Sambora Undivided lyrics © BMG Rights Management, Capitol CMG Publishing, Songtrust Ave, Sony/ATV Music Publishing LLC, Universal Music Publishing Group, Warner Chappell Music, Inc.

Ray Llarena

Nevertheless the foundation of God standeth sure, having this seal, The Lord knoweth them that are his. And, let every one that nameth the name of Christ depart from iniquity. But in a great house there are not only vessels of gold and of silver, but also of wood and of earth; and some to honour, and some to dishonour. If a man therefore purge himself from these, he shall be a vessel unto honour, sanctified, and meet for the master's use, and prepared unto every good work.

2 Timothy 2:19-21

God knows *"them that are his."* Aren't you glad the Lord knows you? Then He calls us to consecration: *"Let everyone that nameth the name of Christ depart from iniquity."* Consecration is departing from everything that is not of God, departing from every appearance of evil. When you consecrate your life to God, you begin to recognize what is unclean, and you remember the Word of the Lord:

Wherefore come out from among them, and be ye separate, saith the Lord, and touch not the unclean thing; and I will receive you.

2 Corinthians 6:17

A Call to Consecration

And have no fellowship with the unfruitful works of darkness, but rather reprove them.

Ephesians 5:11

Be ye not unequally yoked together with unbelievers: for what fellowship hath righteousness with unrighteousness? and what communion hath light with darkness?   2 Corinthians 6:14

We are no longer of the darkness. Therefore, we know the difference between sin and righteousness. We avoid iniquity, sin, wickedness, evil and strive in order to live holy lives. When we take a step toward holiness, that is consecration.

The Bible even tells us:

Abstain from all appearance of evil.

1 Thessalonians 5:22

What does this mean? It means to avoid anything that cannot glorify God, anything that doesn't build up your faith, anything that doesn't enhance your spiritual life, anything that doesn't cultivate a desire for spiritual things. Don't touch it or even smell it or look upon it. Depart from it.

Go away from it or else your heart will be turned away from the Lord.

God forbid the children of Israel from intermarrying with the people of other nations, but that was not racial discrimination. It was because the people of other nations were not people of faith.

Solomon's life had such a wonderful beginning. God blessed him, and God honored him. Then, however, because Solomon married wives who didn't know God, they turned his heart away from God. Reading about Solomon's final days is painful. Here it is from the New International Version of the Bible:

*King Solomon, however, loved many foreign women besides Pharaoh's daughter—Moabites, Ammonites, Edomites, Sidonians and Hittites. They were from nations about which the L*ORD* had told the Israelites, "You must not intermarry with them, because they will surely turn your hearts after their gods." Nevertheless, Solomon held fast to them in love. He had seven hundred wives of royal birth and three hundred concubines, and his wives led him astray. As Solomon grew old, his wives turned his heart after other gods, and his heart was not fully devoted* *to the LORD his God, as the heart of David his father had been. He followed Ashtoreth the goddess of the Sidonians, and Molek the detestable god of the Ammonites. So Solomon did evil in the eyes of the LORD; he did not follow the LORD completely, as David his father had done.*

On a hill east of Jerusalem, Solomon built a high place for Chemosh the detestable god of Moab, and for Molek the detestable god of the Ammonites. He did the same for all his foreign wives, who burned incense and offered sacrifices to their gods.

The LORD became angry with Solomon because his heart had turned away from the LORD, the God of Israel, who had appeared to him twice. Although he had forbidden Solomon to follow other gods, Solomon did not keep the LORD's command.

1 Kings 11:1-10

What a sad ending to a life with so much promise! Sin will turn your heart away from God. Lust will turn your heart away from God. The flesh will turn your heart away from God. The love of money will turn your heart away from God. Pride will turn your heart away from God. Rebellion will turn your heart away from God. Anything that is not of God must be avoided. Paul wrote to the Philippian believers of the first century:

> *Finally, brethren, whatsoever things are true, whatsoever things are honest, whatsoever things are just, whatsoever things are pure, whatsoever things are lovely, whatsoever things are of good report; if there be any virtue, and if there be any praise, think on these things.*   Philippians 4:8

Even our thoughts must be protected. This is a call to consecration. Let us turn away from sin. Say today, "No more! This is the end! I'm burning all the bridges behind me, and I'm going to live for God. Take the whole world, but give me Jesus. There can be no turning back. The world behind me, the cross before me. There can be no turning back."

You and I, beloved, are called to worship God *"in the beauty of holiness":*

> *Give unto the LORD the glory due unto his name: bring an offering, and come before him: worship the LORD in the beauty of holiness.*
> 1 Chronicles 16:29

A Call to Consecration

*Give unto the L*ORD *the glory due unto his name; worship the Lord in the beauty of holiness.*

Psalm 29:2

*O worship the L*ORD *in the beauty of holiness: fear before him, all the earth.*   Psalm 96:9

Paul wrote to Timothy:

But in a great house there are not only vessels of gold and of silver, but also of wood and of earth; and some to honour, and some to dishonour. If a man therefore purge himself from these, he shall be a vessel unto honour, sanctified, and meet for the master's use, and prepared unto every good work.   2 Timothy 2:20-21

This word *sanctified* is almost synonymous with *consecration. Sanctified* means "set aside, separated." Separated for what? *"Sanctified ... for the master's use, and prepared unto every good work."* Being sanctified is being consecrated, separated for God's use.

The psalmist asked the question of the Lord:

Ray Llarena

Lord, who shall abide in thy tabernacle? who shall dwell in thy holy hill? Psalm 15:1

What does it mean? It means who can come into God's presence? Who can come under the shadow of His glory? Who can come into His house? Who can come into His tabernacle? Then, he answered his own question:

He that walketh uprightly, and worketh righteousness, and speaketh the truth in his heart. He that backbiteth not with his tongue, nor doeth evil to his neighbour, nor taketh up a reproach against his neighbour. In whose eyes a vile person is contemned; but he honoureth them that fear the Lord. He that sweareth to his own hurt, and changeth not. He that putteth not out his money to usury, nor taketh reward against the innocent. He that doeth these things shall never be moved. Psalm 15:2-5

Underline these verses in your Bible. Engrave them upon your heart. Here's another one:

Blessed is the man that walketh not in the counsel of the ungodly, nor standeth in the way of sinners,

A Call to Consecration

nor sitter in the seat of the scornful. But his delight is in the law of the LORD; and in his law doth he meditate day and night. And he shall be like a tree planted by the rivers of water, that bringeth forth his fruit in his season; his leaf also shall not wither; and whatsoever he doeth shall prosper. The ungodly are not so: but are like the chaff which the wind driveth away. Therefore the ungodly shall not stand in the judgment, nor sinners in the congregation of the righteous. For the LORD knoweth the way of the righteous: but the way of the ungodly shall perish. Psalm 1:1-6

Who will be blessed? The man or woman who does not partake of the sin of the people around them. Come out from among them. Be one of those who walk uprightly and work righteousness. How can you walk in righteousness if you're not consecrated to the purpose of God?

Psalm 15 also speaks of the one who *"speaketh the truth in his heart."* This is so important to God. To you, what you're saying may be "a little white lie," but to God it represents the first step to Hell! A lie is a lie whether it's brown, black, yellow, white, green, purple, or orange. Whether it's small or it's big, a lie is still a lie.

The Bible tells us that the father of all lies is the devil. Every time you lie, you're saying, "My father is the devil."

Paul wrote:

> *Lie not one to another, seeing that ye have put off the old man with his deeds; and have put on the new man, which is renewed in knowledge after the image of him that created him.*
>
> Colossians 3:9-10

If you have been lying, stop lying. Speak the truth in righteousness. Consecrate your life to God and depart from iniquity. Surrender your life, sanctify your life to God, and speak in truth.

I realize that many of what we call "petty sins" are part of our fallen nature, and everyone seems to be doing it, but God can give you an anointing and strength to overcome sin of every type, big and small. You have the power of God in you that enables you to say "no" to sin.

Why do Christian people sin? Because they love sin. It feels good to them. When you become tired of sinning, you will stop. When you are tired of lying, you will stop lying. When you are tired of the guilt and the feeling of conviction, you will stop sinning.

A Call to Consecration

Exaggerating a story is telling a lie. Blowing things out of proportion is telling a lie. The only way we can stop gossiping and backbiting against others is to consecrate our lives to God and let Him empower us to overcome. Consecrate every member of your body, every faculty that you have, to the Lord. Be sanctified for God. Be separated from the things of the world, and then you will start talking differently.

Why is it that people love to talk about ungodly things? Stop that! That doesn't glorify God. That doesn't enhance His Kingdom. That doesn't build up the Body of Christ. Stop it because it's ungodly and unacceptable to God, and it will not bring you any blessing from Him.

Psalm 15 included in the list: *"nor doeth evil to his neighbour."* You are called to be a witness to unbelievers so that your neighbor will know Jesus Christ through you. Sometimes the reason our neighbors are not saved and we are not leading them to the Lord is that they're not seeing in us the light of Jesus Christ. This is serious.

The next phrase in Psalm 15 is *"nor taketh up a approach against his neighbor."* Are we even saying bad things about our neighbor? How could we ever win them to Christ? Do they think of Christians as hypocrites because of what they see in us? Do they think they are living better lives than those who profess righteousness? May God help us.

Among recent generations, being godly is unpopular. Sinners are the popular ones. The "in" things are drugs, sex, and rock and roll. If you are twenty-five and are still a virgin, you are ridiculed. There must be something wrong with you.

A brother approached me at the close of a service and said, "Pastor, can I see you? I want to discuss something with you."

I said, "Call and make an appointment with my secretary."

He came, we prayed together, and then I said, "Okay, what's the problem, brother?"

He said, "I don't know how to begin, Pastor, but this has really been bothering me. I'm over forty years old, I'm not yet married, and I'm still a virgin."

I said, "Praise the Lord!" It takes guts to keep yourself clean these days. I said, "I'm very proud of you, and I'm delighted. Finally, I have found somebody who is still pure."

"But, Pastor, you don't understand," he began to object. "I'm like this because I have not experienced it."

A Call to Consecration

"Hey," I said, "it's okay. In the eyes of the world, this is very abnormal, but in the eyes of God, it is perfectly normal." The call to consecration is a call to holiness.

Psalm 15 went on to speak of *"he that putteth not out his money to usury nor taketh reward against the innocent. He that doeth these things will not be moved."* Usury refers to lending money at an extravagantly high interest rate, taking advantage of those who need help financially and placing on them an undue burden. The call to consecration is a call to holiness.

Paul used some very strong language when pleading with the Roman believers for consecration:

I beseech you therefore, brethren, by the mercies of God, that ye present your bodies a living sacrifice, holy, acceptable unto God, which is your reasonable service. And be not conformed to this world: but be ye transformed by the renewing of your mind, that ye may prove what is that good, and acceptable, and perfect, will of God. For I say, through the grace given unto me, to every man that is among you, not to think of himself more highly than he ought to think; but to think soberly, according as God hath dealt to every man the measure of faith.   Romans 12:1-3

Bless them which persecute you: bless, and curse not. Rejoice with them that do rejoice, and weep with them that weep. Be of the same mind one toward another. Mind not high things, but condescend to men of low estate. Be not wise in your own conceits. Recompense to no man evil for evil. Provide things honest in the sight of all men. If it be possible, as much as lieth in you, live peaceably with all men.

Dearly beloved, avenge not yourselves, but rather give place unto wrath: for it is written, Vengeance is mine; I will repay, saith the Lord. Therefore if thine enemy hunger, feed him; if he thirst, give him drink: for in so doing thou shalt heap coals of fire on his head. Be not overcome of evil, but overcome evil with good.   Romans 12:14-21

The call to consecration is a call to a life of dedication to God, a life of surrender to the Lord. As believers in Christ, we need to separate ourselves *from* that which is unclean, and we need to separate ourselves *unto* the things of God. We need to depart from every appearance of evil. In this way, we can respond positively to the moving of the Holy Ghost.

Beloved, you know yourself, and you know where you stand with God. Don't try to cover your sin or hide from it. Nothing is hidden from the sight of God. Accept the fact that you need God, you need the anointing of God, you need a touch from God.

We all fall short of the glory of God, and therefore we need to consecrate ourselves afresh and anew. We need to dedicate ourselves, we need to sanctify ourselves, we need to be set apart for God. Let us get out from among those who care not to honor God, for their presence contaminates us with the things of the world.

How are you in the sight of God? How do you stand in the presence of the Lord? How is your heart in His sight? This is a call to consecration.

CHAPTER 2

A CALL TO CONSECRATION: PART 2

The thief cometh not, but for to steal, and to kill, and to destroy: I am come that they might have life, and that they might have it more abundantly.

John 10:10

Consecration is very important, and a call to consecration is almost equivalent to a call to discipleship. You cannot be a disciple of the Lord Jesus Christ unless you are consecrated, committed, and dedicated. And you cannot be dedicated and committed to Christ unless you answer the call to become His disciple. There is a big difference between calling yourself a Christian and being a real disciple of Jesus Christ.

Not all Christians are disciples. I'm not saying that if you're not a disciple, you can't go to Heaven. I'm saying there is another step, a higher step than just being called a Christian. Personally, I don't want to live just barely making it to Heaven. I don't want to live this life struggling and constantly fighting my way to get through. That's not what God wants for us. That's not the kind of life He wants us to enjoy. He has destined us to an abundant life.

Living an abundant life doesn't mean that you will have no more problems. It doesn't mean that the devil will never bother you again. It doesn't mean that you will always be smiling and have no trouble whatsoever. Abundant life means that you can be at peace, you can be at rest, you can smile in spite of the fact that the whole world is collapsing around you. That's abundant life. You can still praise the Lord in spite of the fact that your pocketbook is empty. That's abundant life.

Commitment, consecration, discipleship, and dedication represent a step further from the point of having Jesus as Savior. This step is to make Him Lord and Master of your life. There's a big difference.

We can know God's love, His mercy, His compassion, His forgiveness, His kindness, and His consideration and still not be allowing Him to be Lord and Master of our daily lives. He is our Savior, but is He our Lord?

The Lordship of Jesus Christ in your life is something entirely different. It involves His authority, His power, His government, His rulership, His control, and His supremacy, and it involves our submission, our surrender, and our being willing to be governed, regulated, directed, and guided by Him. This goes far beyond being "goody, goody."

God is good, God is sweet, God is wonderful, and God is great, but in His goodness, sweetness, wonderfulness, and greatness, He calls us to consecration. This is very important.

Until Moses came to the burning bush, he had not seen the manifestation of the power of God, he had not seen the revelation of the glory of God, and he had not known the purpose and the plan of God. Then, suddenly, God said to him, "Take off your shoes."

> *And he said, Draw not nigh hither: put off thy shoes from off thy feet, for the place whereon thou standest is holy ground.* Exodus 3:5

What was God saying? He was saying, "Empty yourself. Remove everything that is ungodly. Remove everything that is of the flesh and of the world. You're standing on holy ground. Therefore, anything that is carnal, remove it, and then you will see My glory."

The anointing of God is powerful, but it's not cheap. His glory is marvelous, but it cannot be handled lightly. It is awesome, powerful, and glorious—out of this world—and it will "blow your mind," but it must be considered sacred, and even more so, holy.

The dictionary says of the word *sacred:* "connected with God (or the gods) or dedicated to a religious purpose and so deserving veneration: holy, hallowed, blessed, blest, consecrated, sanctified, dedicated." Of the word *holy* it says: "dedicated or consecrated to God or a religious purpose: sacred, consecrated, hallowed, sanctified, venerated, revered." God calls upon every man, woman, boy and girl who calls themselves a Christian to consecrate their life to the Master. There is a blessing in consecration.

As we have seen, when there is a separation, a coming out from the things that are of the world and not of God, this opens the door of blessing. We will never have the move of God unless we pay the required price.

Once, when I was in Ecuador, South America for meetings, a friend of mine and I were shopping. I said, "Let's have some fruits." There were fruits in that country which I had never eaten in the U.S., but money was tight, so we were being careful how we spent.

Some who live by faith spend money like it's going out of style. I am more reserved. Yes, we walk by faith, but we're not stupid or crazy. We need to be wise.

I looked at one fruit, and it looked good. "How much is that?" I asked.

"Well, in American money, that's fifty cents," he said.

At the time, fifty cents seemed like a lot of money. I had three more weeks to go on my trip, so I moved on to another fruit. "How much is that one?" I asked.

"Twenty-five cents in American money," he said.

"Good," I said, "I'll take it."

"I'll get it," my friend said, and he paid.

We bought the fruit and walked on. As we were walking and eating, I suddenly discovered that the fruit we had bought was not much of a bargain, "Oh, my goodness," I said to him, "it's half rotten."

"What did you expect to get for twenty-five cents?" he responded.

What am I saying? I'm saying that you get what you're willing to pay for. If you want more of God, you need to pay the price.

I learned a lesson many years ago about shopping: If you really need something, you really want it, and you really like it, don't look at the price tag. Just pay the price, take it home, and be happy with it.

I'm not saying that you go out there and spend lavishly using your credit cards. Some of you need to cut those up and throw them away. Being debt free is a wonderful feeling, and plastic cards have made spending far too easy for many. Some of you buy things that stay in the closet for years, and you've forgotten about them long before you have them paid off.

Now, let's get back to the subject. When it comes to the things of God, it's the same principle. You get what you're willing to pay for. If you only pray five minutes at a time, you will get five minutes worth of blessing.

Consecration is very important. It's a demand and a requirement for a fruitful Christian life. Few things are more important in life.

Consecration means dedicating your life solely for the purpose of God. Another word for it is *sanctification*. What does it mean to be sanctified? It simply means "to be set apart." The overhead projectors we use in church cannot be removed and used for any other purpose. They are set apart for that sole purpose and have no other use. You and I need to be set apart, separated, pulled out from among the crowd for one unique purpose, to glorify God here on earth. That was our intended purpose from the moment of creation, so we must be sanctified, set apart for God.

The children of Israel were called of God to be a nation separated from the rest of the world, so God told them not to intermarry with other nationalities. Intermarriage with unbelievers would defile them. As a nation, Israel continued to progress and advance. Then, at times, God even began to separate them one tribe from other tribes. Why? Because He knew that there was too much contamination in those other tribes.

The Tabernacle in the wilderness had fences or curtains that kept certain people out. In some areas, only the priest was allowed in, and he had to undergo strict rules of purity. In other areas, only the Levites could come in, and they were a tribe set apart for service to God. The Tabernacle was a holy place, sanctified and set apart for the specific purpose of being a meeting place for God and His people and must not be contaminated.

This was the place where God's glory would be revealed, the place from which the Word of God would come forth. Only in this place would the Shekinah glory of God be seen, and only in this place would certain other manifestations of the supernatural power of the Lord be experienced.

Anyone who dared enter unworthily into certain parts of this building would be struck dead. Anyone who, without the proper authorization, preparation and training, touched or even looked upon the Ark of the Covenant and the Mercy Seat would immediately die.

Two of Aaron's sons, who were themselves Levites and, therefore, entitled to be in the presence of God, got themselves into serious trouble by offering to God something that was not acceptable, something that was not sanctified, something that was not consecrated, something that was not holy.

The Bible called their offering *"strange fire"* (Leviticus 10:1). It was strange because it was not sanctioned by God. And what happened? Verse 2 declares:

> *And there went out fire from the LORD, and devoured them, and they died before the LORD.*

A Call to Consecration

Nadab and Abihu may have been sons of the High Priest, but they died because that holy place was consecrated and separated to the glory of God. It was sanctified and set apart only for the purpose of worshiping God, honoring God, glorifying God, and carrying out the program of God. It was a place for fulfilling the plan of God, and that plan was to meet His people and communicate to them His mind, His purpose, His will, and His direction.

If you compromise your stand with God with the things of the world, it will be difficult for you to find God's will for your life. If you cannot sanctify yourself, set yourself apart, removing yourself from anything that is not of God, it will be difficult for you to find the will of God.

There were people in the Bible (and there are people today) who fasted for long periods of time just to say they were fasting. Today some boast of even fasting for forty days, like Jesus did. Most of those who fasted in the Bible days would separate themselves from the busy schedule of life and go into a desert place where they could pray without distractions. In this way, they were sanctified, separating themselves for the purpose of hearing the voice of God and for the purpose of seeing the manifestations of God and knowing and under-standing the direction of God for their lives.

Genesis 13 records the separation of Lot and Abraham, his nephew. Lot moved himself and his family closer to the cities of Sodom and Gomorrah, while Abraham chose to remain more isolated from such places. The very last verses of that chapter tell us:

> *And the LORD said unto Abram, after that Lot was separated from him, Lift up now thine eyes, and look from the place where thou art northward, and southward, and eastward, and westward: for all the land which thou seest, to thee will I give it, and to thy seed for ever. And I will make thy seed as the dust of the earth: so that if a man can number the dust of the earth, then shall thy seed also be numbered. Arise, walk through the land in the length of it and in the breadth of it; for I will give it unto thee. Then Abram removed his tent, and came and dwelt in the plain of Mamre, which is in Hebron, and built there an altar unto the LORD.*
>
> Genesis 13:14-18

It was there, in that separated place, that Abraham heard the voice of God, and what he heard was glorious. When you consecrate your life to God, when you sanctify yourself, setting yourself apart, you, too, will experience the glory of God. You will find your direction. You will find your purpose in life. You will see the plan of God, and, with His help, you will find your way to victory. When we compromise, letting down our standard a little here and there, it leaves us in a state of confusion.

The first two chapters of Daniel record the fact that this young man was taken prisoner out of the land and carried away to Babylon as a slave. He had lost all rights and was forced to obey the will of his captors. But in time, the king of Babylon learned that Daniel was from royal blood, and that changed everything.

You are also of royal blood, the blood of the King of Kings and the Lord of Lords, Jesus Christ. You have been adopted into the family of God, and your name is written in the Lamb's Book of Life. Through Jesus, you have become a partaker of the divine nature and have received the inheritance of the saints. We are now kings and priests unto God, and He has ordained us to reign with Him.

Would God entrust His authority and ability to those who are not sanctified, set apart, or consecrated? Kings have amazing power. Their word is the law. What they speak affects everyone in the realm. They have to be serious people, dedicated to their unique role in life.

When King Nebuchadnezzar learned that Daniel was of the royal family, he ordered him to be set apart from the other Hebrew slaves. He knew that even if Daniel was not from the royal blood of Babylon, as a royal, he would have dignity. Royals act differently than the common people. Since we are royalty, we must not conduct ourselves like the ordinary citizens of the land. We must behave like the royalty we are.

If I know that my daddy is the owner of everything, I won't act like a slave. I will know that I am set apart, sanctified, consecrated, to rule.

We are also priests unto God here on earth. Do we behave like priests? We have been set apart to demonstrate the glory of God on one hand and the majesty and authority of God on the other. No demon in Hell can stop us from advancing. Yes, we need to consecrate our lives. We need to set ourselves apart.

A Call to Consecration

King Nebuchadnezzar said to his caretaker, "Give these young men the best food. Whatever I am eating, whatever is on my table, serve it to them too."

To Daniel, this was his opportunity. No one was watching, and no one would report him to a superior. With no one around to judge, he could indulge himself a bit, tasting what the world of Babylon was all about. It always starts with a little bite. Big things always start out as small things.

As we grow older, we begin to think about retirement. Personally, I have no plan to retire. As long as I can stand, I will preach until I drop.

But planning for the future is not a bad thing. If you were to put $100 a month into a retirement plan, by the time you retire, you could have more than $1 million to live on. In thirty years you can accumulate half a million in retirement benefits. The same is true about accumulating benefits in Heaven. Every little bit adds up over time.

Heaven is a wonderful place. The streets are paved with gold, and the gates are made of pearl. There is a mansion there built just for you, and it is beyond comparison with all of the palaces and castles built by men.

Ray Llarena

When they offered Daniel the opportunity to eat the king's food, he refused. "No," he said, "I have sanctified myself, I have consecrated myself, I have set myself apart, and so I cannot touch food like that."

Remember, this was an order from the king, and if you disobeyed the orders of the king, you could be killed. You could lose your head and quickly.

So, what did Daniel do? He stuck to his decision and said, "No, just give me bread and vegetables."

Daniel was not really a vegetarian, but this was his decision, and with it, a remarkable thing happened. At the end of ten days, Daniel was visibly more healthy than those who ate at the king's table.

You can indulge yourself on the things of the world, but you will have difficulty sleeping when you go to bed at night. Why? Because of guilt and condemnation. You might partake of the things of the world, but afterward you will not be able to look your pastor in the eyes. Why? Because you know that sometimes he has a word of discernment or a word of knowledge or wisdom, and you know what the Scriptures teach:

Be sure your sin will find you out.
Numbers 32:23

A Call to Consecration

So, what do you do? You begin to absent yourself from the fellowship of other believers. You know that when you're among people of God, where two or three are gathered together in His name, He is there in the midst of them, and when He is in the midst, there will be conviction, and the Holy Spirit will be dealing with your heart. Then, before long, you find yourself out of fellowship with God, out of fellowship with the church, and on your way to Hell.

There's a sign at railroad crossings. It says, "Stop, Look, Listen," and wise people understand what that means. Crossing those tracks is a dangerous undertaking and must be approached with caution.

You will be healthier and will live longer if you refuse to indulge in the things of this world. Self-control is a must for any believer. Control your appetite, and you will not have to worry about losing weight. You will not be worried about how you can get to aerobics class after you have gained too many inches around the waist.

Did you know that gluttony is a sin? Many believers don't seem to know this. Overeating is a sin, and a great many of our physical problems come from eating too much or eating the wrong things. Today, most Christians are more adept at feasting than they are at fasting. There are more church banquets than there are prayer meetings. And we wonder why we don't have revival! Our bellies are fat, but our spirits are so skinny that Satan can blow us away. Self-control is a part of our consecration to God.

In John 17, we have recorded a lengthy prayer that Jesus prayed. Part of that prayer says:

> *I pray not that thou shouldest take them out of the world, but that thou shouldest keep them from the evil. They are not of the world, even as I am not of the world. Sanctify them through thy truth: thy word is truth. As thou hast sent me into the world, even so have I also sent them into the world. And for their sakes I sanctify myself, that they also might be sanctified through the truth.* John 17:15-18

That was what Jesus prayed for His disciples. This was His desire. He did not pray for them to be taken out of the world; He prayed that the Father would keep them from the world's evils. God will not take you out of your problems; He will show you how to overcome them. He will not take you out of your predicament, but He *will* keep you from the evil one.

A Call to Consecration

Who is the evil one mentioned here? Satan. We are more than conquerors over him.

Jesus said that we are *"not of the world."* Can you say that? He was *"not of the world,"* and that should be our testimony too. Then He prayed for us: *"Sanctify them through thy truth; thy word is truth."* So, the prayer of Jesus, the heart desire of Jesus was not that we should be taken out of the world, but that we should willingly renounce the world and its passions and choose, instead, to live for God in this world.

During our times of temptation, God is not powerless. He's right there with us, and He can keep us from the influence of the evil one. Usually, He will not take you out of your situation. Instead, He will give you grace to endure it and strength and power to stand against it. He will give you the ability to exercise your authority as a king, to rule and subdue all dominion and principalities and power that are standing against you. You are a king, so take charge and rule your world.

This truth is simple and yet very profound. You have been sanctified and consecrated to rule. Now, begin ruling.

What does a king do when there is another kingdom trying to seize his country? He calls his commander in chief and tells him to prepare the army and go on the attack.

I've never played football, but I understand there is what is called offense and defense. Most of the time we Christians are just defensive. As long as we're holding our fort, the enemy can't come in. But, at the same time, we're not gaining any ground. Maybe we're not loosing, but we're also not winning. The sad thing is that many believers, after many years, are still in the same place spiritually. Could this be because they are only playing defense? Let's take the offensive, push the devil back, and gain ground for God.

What did God say about it? He said that anyplace we touch will be our inheritance. When England became such a powerful kingdom, it was not through defense. Yes, defense is important, but the British set out on a course of conquest, and eventually ruled a vast portion of the earth. National Geographic reported:

> At its height in 1922, it [the British Empire] was the largest empire the world had ever seen, covering around a quarter of Earth's land surface and ruling over 458 million people.

A Call to Consecration

How was this possible? Because the British set themselves to conquer. Therefore, their authority and rulership expanded as far as they were willing to go. The prayer of Jesus showed His deep desire that we would nor give in to this world, but, rather, overcome it.

Paul wrote to the Colossian believers:

If ye then be risen with Christ, seek those things which are above, where Christ sitteth on the right hand of God.   Colossians 3:1

Where is Christ sitting? On the right hand of God? Where is God's throne? In Heaven. Ephesians 2 tells us that we are seated together with Christ in heavenly places:

And you hath he quickened, who were dead in trespasses and sins; wherein in time past ye walked according to the course of this world, according to the prince of the power of the air, the spirit that now worketh in the children of disobedience: among whom also we all had our conversation in times past in the lusts of our flesh, fulfilling the desires of the flesh and of the mind; and were by nature the children of wrath, even as others. But God, who is rich in mercy, for his great love wherewith he loved us, even when we were dead in sins, hath quickened us together with Christ, (by grace ye are saved;) and hath raised us up together, and made us sit together in heavenly places in Christ Jesus: that in the ages to come he might shew the exceeding riches of his grace in his kindness toward us through Christ Jesus.

Ephesians 2:1-7

We are already citizens of Heaven, and we have a place reserved for us there. The Bible tells us:

Thus saith the Lord, The heaven is my throne, and the earth is my footstool: where is the house that ye build unto me? and where is the place of my rest? Isaiah 66:1

God rules over all. Heaven is His throne, but Earth is His footstool. Jesus taught us to pray:

Thy kingdom come, Thy will be done in earth, as it is in heaven. Matthew 6:10

A Call to Consecration

Now, Paul is teaching us that since we are risen with Christ, we should *"seek those things which are above."* The next verse concludes:

> *Set your affection on things above, not on things on the earth.*　　　　　Colossians 3:2

What does it mean? What is our *"affection"*? It is our desire, our love, our craving, our longing, our appetite, and it is to be fixed on things above, not on things on the earth.

> *This world is not my home, I'm just a-passing through,*
> *My treasures are laid up somewhere beyond the blue;*
> *The angels beckon me from Heaven's open door,*
> *And I can't feel at home in this world anymore.*[1]

Jesus said:

> *Let not your heart be troubled: ye believe in God, believe also in me. In my Father's house are many mansions: if it were not so, I would have told you. I go to prepare a place for you. And if I go and pre-pare a place for you, I will come again, and receive*

---

1. Author Unknown, Public Domain

you unto myself; that where I am, there ye may be
also.   John 14:1-3

If Heaven is your goal, then get your affections set on Heaven and heavenly things now. Focus your desire on that heavenly home. Jesus taught us:

No man, having put his hand to the plough, and
looking back, is fit for the kingdom of God.
                                        Luke 9:62

Would you dare to drive while looking backward? That would be suicide. Well, if you're really going to Heaven, start longing for Heaven. Put your desire on Heaven. Put your dream on Heaven. Put your mind on Heaven. Let your spirit be reaching out to Heaven. Set your desires on things above where Christ is.

The next verse explains how we can do it:

For ye are dead, and your life is hid with Christ
in God.   Colossians 3:3

Verse 4 is powerful too:

A Call to Consecration

When Christ, who is our life, shall appear, then shall ye also appear with him in glory.

Colossians 3:4

Underline verses 5 and 6 in you Bible. They say:

Mortify therefore your members which are upon the earth; fornication, uncleanness, inordinate affection, evil concupiscence, and covetousness, which is idolatry: for which things' sake the wrath of God cometh on the children of disobedience. In the which ye also walked some time, when ye lived in them.

Colossians 3:5-7

"Inordinate affection" is a nice way of saying homosexuality. Yes, homosexuality is an "inordinate affection." What does mortify mean? It means to kill. Mortify it. Clean it up. Sanctify your members. Consecrate your members. Cut off all those things that are not of God.

Why must you mortify your members which are upon the earth? Because you're on your way to Heaven. You are risen together with Christ. You are seated together with Him in heavenly places. You are now under the rulership, the government and the authority of Christ.

What are we to mortify or kill? Fornication, uncleanness, inordinate affection, evil concupiscence and covetousness, which is idolatry, *"for which things sake the wrath of God cometh upon the children of disobedience."*

These are not my words; they are God's words. If they make you angry and you're offended, talk to God. I'm just saying what God is saying in His Word.

If you're committing adultery, you're not sanctifying yourself. If you're committing fornication, you're not sanctifying yourself. If you're living in idolatry or are covetous, you're not sanctifying yourself. If you're practicing homosexuality, you're not sanctifying yourself to God. You're not setting yourself apart from things that are ungodly and unholy. If things you are doing are not with virtue, not with praise, not of good report, not honest, then they are not pleasing to God. Get them out of your life or risk losing Heaven.

We are to avoid even the very appearance of evil. Run from it.

If you are lying, lie no more (see Colossians 3:9). If you are stealing, steal no more (see Ephesians 4:28).

A Call to Consecration

If you are gossiping, gossip no more (see 1 Timothy 5:13). And if you are not paying your tithes, you're a thief of the worst kind, for you're robbing God (see Malachi 3:8).

Are you doing none of those things but are not fully following the Lord? It's called disobedience, and God calls it out:

> *And Samuel said, Hath the LORD as great delight in burnt offerings and sacrifices, as in obeying the voice of the LORD? Behold, to obey is better than sacrifice, and to hearken than the fat of rams.*
>
> 1 Samuel 15:22

Can God receive your offering? Not if you are living in disobedience. He doesn't take pleasure in a hypocritical sacrifice. If you are grumbling and murmuring and not giving out of your heart, that is unacceptable to God. He doesn't need your money; He needs your obedience. Jesus said:

> *If ye love me, keep my commandments.*
>
> John 14:15

We must keep God's words, submit to His words, and follow His words. Some use God's money to buy gifts for their friends. Be careful! Don't be guilty of giving to others what belongs to God. You are in covenant with Him. If you keep your part of the covenant, you will never have to worry about God keeping His. He has promised so many blessings that there will not be enough room to contain them (see Malachi 3:10).

Are you giving God the time He deserves? Are you faithful to the House of God?

And let us consider one another to provoke unto love and to good works: not forsaking the assembling of ourselves together, as the manner of some is; but exhorting one another: and so much the more, as ye see the day approaching.

Hebrews 10:24-25

We are to honor the Lord's Day. Doing so will benefit you, enhancing your life spiritually and physically. Set your affection on things that are above. Beginning with verse 8, Paul gives us a list of things that are harmful to the Christian life and the contrast of what our lives should look like:

A Call to Consecration

But now ye also put off all these; anger, wrath, malice, blasphemy, filthy communication out of your mouth. Lie not one to another, seeing that ye have put off the old man with his deeds; and have put on the new man, which is renewed in knowledge after the image of him that created him: where there is neither Greek nor Jew, circumcision nor uncircumcision, Barbarian, Scythian, bond nor free: but Christ is all, and in all.

Put on therefore, as the elect of God, holy and beloved, bowels of mercies, kindness, humbleness of mind, meekness, longsuffering; forbearing one another, and forgiving one another, if any man have a quarrel against any: even as Christ forgave you, so also do ye. Colossians 3:8-13

Now that you are a Christian, now that you are a disciple of Christ, now that you are a believer, now that you are consecrating yourself, now that you are sanctifying yourself, now that you are dedicating yourself to be holy for the purposes of God, you must *"put off these things."* You can do it with God's help. Just as God said to Moses, "Remove your shoes, for you are standing on holy ground," He says to you today, *"Put off all these things."*

63

What is *"filthy communication?"* Anything that does not glorify God, anything that cannot build up your faith, anything that cannot serve a spiritual purpose in your life,

Just as important as the list of "put-offs" is the list of "put-ons." *"Put on therefore, as the elect of God."* That's you. God said:

> *Ye have not chosen me, but I have chosen you, and ordained you, that ye should go and bring forth fruit, and that your fruit should remain: that whatsoever ye shall ask of the Father in my name, he may give it you.* John 15:16

You are the called, the chosen, the elect, and He who called you, chose you, and elected you is holy. *"Put on therefore, as the elect of God, holy and beloved ... ."* Beloved, we need to consecrate ourselves as children of the living God.

These next few verses of Colossians are critical:

> *And above all these things put on charity, which is the bond of perfectness. And let the peace of God rule in your hearts, to the which also ye are called in one body; and be ye thankful. Let the word of*

A Call to Consecration

Christ dwell in you richly in all wisdom; teaching and admonishing one another in psalms and hymns and spiritual songs, singing with grace in your hearts to the Lord. And whatsoever ye do in word or deed, do all in the name of the Lord Jesus, giving thanks to God and the Father by him.

Colossians 3:14-17

After that, Paul gets down to practical everyday matters: the relationship between husbands and wives, the relationship between parents and their children, our relationship with the world around us. In everything we do, we are to glorify the Lord. The section concludes with these powerful words:

And whatsoever ye do, do it heartily, as to the Lord, and not unto men; knowing that of the Lord ye shall receive the reward of the inheritance: for ye serve the Lord Christ. But he that doeth wrong shall receive for the wrong which he hath done: and there is no respect of persons.

Colossians 3:23-25

"Whatsoever ye do." Our new life in Christ should affect our every word and action, and everything

we do and say should be done *"as to the Lord."* When you are consecrated, when you are dedicated, when you are sanctified, you could care less whether you are recognized, honored, or patted on the back. All that matters is to have and to spread the glory of God. We need God, we need His anointing, we need His miracle-working power, and we need His favor in our lives. Therefore, we will not touch, taste, or handle things that are not of Him. We will obey the admonition:

> *Come out from among them, and be ye separate, saith the Lord, and touch not the unclean thing; and I will receive you.* 2 Corinthians 6:17

Can you see the clear condition that God has placed on us here? Before He can be our Father and our God, we need to come out from among the ungodly, be separate, and touch not the unclean thing.

We need to sanctify ourselves. We need to consecrate ourselves. We need to cleanse ourselves. When you are consecrated to God, your heart will be pure and clean, and your affection will be set on things above.

A Call to Consecration

Don't be influenced by people around you. Listen to the Word of God, obey the Word of God, and respond to the Word of God. Set yourself apart and stop everything you are doing that cannot increase God's anointing in your life. Stop going places that are not helping you to grow spiritually. This is a call to consecration.

CHAPTER 3

A CALL TO CONSECRATION: PART 3

Giving thanks unto the Father, which hath made us meet to be partakers of the inheritance of the saints in light: who hath delivered us from the power of darkness, and hath translated us into the kingdom of his dear Son.   Colossians 1:12-13

God is calling us to consecrate our lives to Him, surrendering our all to His lordship. As we have seen, we, as believers in Christ, must separate ourselves from things that are not godly, cutting off our association with all evil. Why? Because there can be no fellowship between light and darkness.

When you are born again and you receive Jesus as your Lord and Savior, it is difficult to "hang out" with people you are accustomed to "hanging out" with. You have different desires now. You have a different outlook on life. Your nature is changed. If you continue to hang around with your old friends and do the same things you've been doing with them, it will inevitably bring you back to the same bondages you were delivered from.

I'm not saying you cannot be friends with those people. You *can* be friends, but from a certain distance, and your purpose in maintaining the relationship is winning them to the Lord. You cannot be as closely associated with sinners as you were before you got saved.

The life of a Christian is a life of total separation. Being a disciple, being a follower of Jesus Christ, means being born into a totally new Kingdom. We have passed from death unto life and been translated from darkness to light.

This word *translated* means to be taken from one place and transferred or placed somewhere else. We have been translated from the kingdom of darkness to the Kingdom of light, so that we are no longer what we used to be.

This doesn't all happen at one time. This life of consecration is a progressive work of grace, a progressive work of the Holy Spirit, bringing us into a place of purification, bringing us through a process of cleansing. We are transformed from glory to glory and from faith to faith.

A Call to Consecration

We are being renewed constantly by the power of God's Word and by the operation of the Holy Spirit in our lives. He is pruning us, purging us, and cleansing us, so that we will grow in Him and so the Christ that is in us might be revealed and manifested outwardly. This is very important so that the people around us can see that inner working of God's Spirit and the result of the power of God moving in us, transforming us.

We are changed by God, and that is the greatest testimony anyone can have: "I've been changed. I've been transformed. I've been renewed. I once was blind, but now I see. I once was lost, but now I'm found. I once was in bondage, but now I'm set free. I was on my way to Hell, but now I'm on my way to Heaven shouting victory."

A marriage between a husband and wife who have a superficial relationship will not last. Before two people get married, they need to be sure they are ready for a lifetime of commitment. Through thick and thin, they must maintain their commitment. Through high water and low water, earthquakes, tornadoes, darkness, blizzards, snowstorms, they must remain committed to each other. The moment you received Christ as the Lord of your life, you made a commitment to Him, and He made a commitment to you. Don't let anything or anyone hinder that commitment.

I want to share a few things that are involved in our life of consecration to God. The Bible tells us that we will be purified by fire. Your faith will be tried or tested. God's purpose in this testing is not to destroy you, but to purify you, so that you come forth as pure gold.

There are sufferings in the Christian life. These are trials of your faith. You cannot receive an award until you have passed the test, just as you cannot receive a trophy until you have won the race. Your Christianity cannot be true Christianity if you have not yet been tested. It is in your testing, in your trials, that you discover the substance and the reality of your relationship with Jesus Christ. If, after the trials are over, after the storms have passed, after the suffering is ended, your relationship with the Lord Jesus Christ is still in tact, that's genuine salvation. That is true eternal life. That is real faith. That is complete trust. That is consecration.

You cannot be consecrated unless you have first been justified. *Justification* is a judicial term. If you have been charged with a crime, you might be arrested, brought to jail, and eventually put on trial. A jury might be convened to decide your fate. Other people might make their judgments based on what they know. We know what the Bible says:

For the wages of sin is death.   Romans 6:23

You and I are guilty and, therefore, merit the wages of sin, which is death. The beautiful thing is expressed in the rest of that verse. Thank God it didn't stop there. It goes on to say:

But the gift of God is eternal life through Jesus Christ our Lord.

I'm so glad that verse didn't stop with death. What I want to emphasize is that we have all been found guilty and we have all been condemned, sentenced to die because of our crime. Then, however, Someone paid for our crime. Someone took our blame upon Himself. Someone bore our sin.

It's almost like the story of the two brothers who were twins. They looked exactly alike, but one of them was a Christian and served the Lord, while the other was living a life of sin involving drugs, sex, and crime. One day, because of his drug habit, the brother living in sin killed a man to get his money. He ran home with the blood of that man on his shirt and pants.

When a policeman came to the scene of the crime, he was told who had done the murder, they learned his address, and someone went to arrest him.

Meanwhile, the sinful brother had said to his Christian twin, "I just committed a terrible crime. I killed someone, and the police are sure to come for me. What am to do?"

The Christian really loved his twin brother, so he said to him, "Don't worry. Go get cleaned up. Change your shirt and pants, and if anyone comes, don't say a thing."

The sinful twin went to the bathroom and cleaned himself up. He took off all his clothes and went to put on clean ones. While he was putting on the clean clothes, the Christian brother found the bloody shirt and pants and put them on. When the policeman arrived, he was arrested. After all, he was found with the evidence on him.

The other brother was about to say, "He's not the one who committed the crime; it's me," but the

Christian brother said, "What other evidence do you need?" And they led him away.

The guilty twin was justified because someone took his sin. He now stood innocent, just as if he had never sinned. He escaped a conviction for murder because someone who loved him took his place.

That's exactly what Jesus Christ did for you and me. He who knew no sin became sin for us so that His righteousness might be imparted unto us:

> *For he hath made him to be sin for us, who knew no sin; that we might be made the righteousness of God in him.* 2 Corinthians 5:21

Yes, you and I stand innocent and righteous now, no longer guilty, no longer condemned for the crimes we committed. We have been justified, just as if we had never sinned, and all because Someone took our blame and bore the penalty for us.

Jesus was *"numbered with the transgressors"* for us (Isaiah 53:12). God the Father laid upon Him *"the iniquities of us all"* (verse 6), and because Jesus willingly bore our shame, we have been justified. We have been set free.

Justification means that we are now free from all condemnation, and this is one of the greatest benefits to living a life of consecration. Condemnation comes when we know we're not doing what we are supposed to do. We are not in a right position in our relationship with God. And nobody needs to tell us that. We know it.

Being justified means that we are declared no longer guilty. The evidence of our crimes was there, but somehow we have been pardoned. Someone took our blame and suffered the penalty in our place. Therefore, we are justified, set free, and delivered from the past. Our debt has been paid in full, and we are free to go. There is no pending balance whatsoever. Our arrest record has been stamped in the red of Jesus' blood:

PAID IN FULL!

Being justified means that we have been restored back to our rightful position of sonship and are now heirs of the Kingdom of God. We have been restored to fellowship and relationship with God Himself. As Paul wrote:

A Call to Consecration

Therefore being justified by faith, we have peace with God through our Lord Jesus Christ: by whom also we have access by faith into this grace wherein we stand, and rejoice in hope of the glory of God. And not only so, but we glory in tribulations also: knowing that tribulation worketh patience; and patience, experience; and experience, hope: and hope maketh not ashamed; because the love of God is shed abroad in our hearts by the Holy Ghost which is given unto us. Romans 5:1-5

Yes, we are justified by faith. Faith in what? Faith in the finished work of Calvary. Faith in what? Faith in the blood of Jesus Christ, the Lamb of God, which *"taketh away the sin of the world"* (John 1:19). Faith in what? Faith in the promise of God. We, therefore, now have *"peace with God through our Lord Jesus Christ."*

The two greatest problems among humanity today are fear and a lack of peace. You can be the poorest man on the face of the earth, but if you have nothing to fear, you have more than the rich man who lives in constant fear. You might even be a homeless person, having no place to go, but if you have peace of mind, the peace that brings joy to your heart, you are better off than a man living in fear in a mansion or a palace.

No wonder the Bible tells us:

And the peace of God, which passeth all understanding, shall keep your hearts and minds through Christ Jesus. Philippians 4:7

The devil will come to disturb you, to trouble you, but Christ will give you the peace that passes all human understanding. You can only have this kind of peace if you have been justified.

In the prisons, especially on death row, and especially when the time of execution is getting closer, there is no peace. You and I are justified through Jesus Christ, and we have received the peace of God. Thank God for that!

There are two kinds of peace. There is the peace *of* God, and there is a peace *with* God. You can never have the peace *of* God until you have peace *with* God. We were all enemies, running from God, and we had no peace. Now we are God's friends, and peace is our portion. Hallelujah!

It is because of justification that a door has been opened for us to come into the presence of God. We now have access to Him because of Jesus' sacrifice. He said:

A Call to Consecration

I am the way, the truth, and the life: no man cometh unto the Father, but by me.   John 14:6

Then said Jesus unto them again, Verily, verily, I say unto you, I am the door of the sheep. All that ever came before me are thieves and robbers: but the sheep did not hear them. I am the door: by me if any man enter in, he shall be saved, and shall go in and out, and find pasture.   John 10:7-9

Jesus is the Door. Therefore we have access to the Father. We have an entryway. We have privileges. We have opportunity. What a blessing it is! Thank God! How can we not determine to be consecrated to God when we have such privileges and such blessings?

Think about this. In the Old Testament, all the Levites were envious of Aaron, the High Priest. He was the only one who was allowed to have access to the very presence of God. Only the High Priest could enter into the Most Holy Place and, thus, enter into the presence of God and into the anointing and blessing of God and into fellowship with God. The rest of the Levites, including those who served as priests, had to stand outside waiting. And yet you and I, by faith, are justified. There is an open door for us. *"Whosoever"* may now enter in. What a blessing!

The veil of the Temple has been rent in twain, and a way has been opened into that Holy Place so that anyone can now go in. But we can only progress into that Holy Place of God's presence if we continually mortify the deeds of the flesh and sanctify ourselves, consecrating our lives to God.

Once you have tasted of the goodness of God, once you have tasted the presence of the Lord, once you have experienced God, you will say, as the young people do, it is "out of this world." Yes, it's super. It's great. The truth is that we don't have enough adjectives to describe it.

Verse 2 of Romans 5 confirms that it is through Jesus that *"we have access by faith into this grace."* What is grace? It's the favor of God. When you are applying for a job, you're nervous. If the interviewer gives you a mean look, you're even more nervous. If he smiles at you, that relaxes you. You and I are able to enter into the favor of God, not because of who we are, but because Jesus took our place and justified us. His action caused us to be acquitted from our crime.

Yes, the Bible tells us:

A Call to Consecration

All have sinned and come short of the glory of God.
Romans 3:23

But in the last part of verse 2, Romans 5 says, *"...and rejoice in hope of the glory of God."* How can we not pay the price to sanctify ourselves and consecrate our lives wholly to God when there is such great glory awaiting us? Verse 3 says, *"Not only so but we glory in tribulation also."* Even after you have been saved, after you are born again, after you have surrendered your life to the Lord, after you've given your complete being, your complete self, to God, there will always be temptation.

Temptation will never stop. Suffering will never stop. It will only stop when we are ushered into Glory. While we are here, we will be tempted, we will go through tribulation, and we will go through hardship. The more you sanctify yourself, the more you consecrate yourself, the more the devil will fight you, and God will allow it so that you can be even more sanctified. The beautiful thing is this: in this world we shall of tribulation, but Jesus added some words:

In the world ye shall have tribulation: but be of good cheer; I have overcome the world.
John 16:33

We can rejoice because Jesus has overcome the world.

The Bible tells us:

> *Blessed are they which are persecuted for righteousness' sake: for theirs is the kingdom of heaven.* Matthew 5:10

Some people feel persecuted because they have done something foolish. To me, thats not persecution and doesn't merit blessing. Jesus was speaking of being *"persecuted for righteousness' sake."* That's what brings promise of blessing. We are even to *"glory in tribulations"* (see Romans 5:3). Tribulation, any tribulation, has a purpose. For one, *"tribulation worketh patience"* (same verse).

We need patience with the process of sanctification. We want it to be over quickly, but it doesn't happen that way. It takes time.

Paul continued in Roman 5:

> *But God commendeth his love toward us, in that, while we were yet sinners, Christ died for us. Much more then, being now justified by his blood, we shall be saved from wrath through him.*

A Call to Consecration

For if, when we were enemies, we were reconciled to God by the death of his Son, much more, being reconciled, we shall be saved by his life.

Romans 5:8-10

That says it all, doesn't it? And it doesn't stop there:

And not only so, but we also joy in God through our Lord Jesus Christ, by whom we have now received the atonement. Romans 5:11

We have received the atonement, the payment, the payoff, the price, the ransom. What is a ransom? It is money paid in exchange for the life of someone who has been abducted, kidnapped, or captured. Our atonement came through faith in the work of the Lord Jesus Christ on Calvary. We are justified by the ransom of His own blood. The result is that we have peace *with* God; we have the peace *of* God. We have access to the throne of God, we have received the grace of God, we have the hope of God, we have the joy of God, and we are enjoying, even now, the glory of God.

The more you consecrate your life, the more you dedicate your life, the more love, the more peace, the more grace, the more joy, the more hope, and the more glory will come to you.

Because we have been justified, we have also been acquitted. That's not the end. We come now to the next term, which is as big as the first one. It is *sanctification*. How does sanctification taste? It tastes like peanut butter in between two pieces of bread with jam and banana. That's my favorite snack. Have you ever tried that? It's so good.

The root word of *sanctification* means "to sanctify," to set apart. Anther word for *sanctify* is *mortify*, and another one is *purify*. You cannot really consecrate your life to God until you sanctify your life.

Who saved you? Jesus, right? There was nothing that you could have done to bring about your salvation. It only comes by the grace of God, and it is all Jesus all the way. Your good works, your righteousness were just like filthy rags in the sight of God. Your salvation was an absolute work of God. Only He could do that.

Sanctification, on the other hand, has a lot more to do with your decisions in life. At some point, you must decide, "I will stop sinning." You have been following the dictates of your flesh, and you have to make the decision to crucify that flesh. You have to draw a line and say, "Enough is enough! I will be different from today."

You cannot ask the Lord to do it all. It is dependent upon your will, and He cannot violate your will. He paid the price to justify you, but now you need to sanctify yourself. Who must mortify the deeds of the flesh? I am the one. Who must die to self? I am the one. Who must be buried with Christ? I am the one. Sanctification means "separation," and I am the only one who can separate myself from wrongdoing.

Numbers records the story of a man named Korah. He rose up against Moses and opposed him, and convinced other community leaders to join him in challenging Moses.

For his part, Moses didn't have much to say. At first, he just prayed. Then he suggested that they meet the next morning and let God resolve the matter.

The next day, Moses told the people to separate themselves from Korah and the other rebellious ones. Those who were on Korah's side should go nearer to his tent. There was a line drawn, a separation made, a cut-off point. And then what happened? The earth opened up and swallowed up Korah alive and all who supported him. There was a sanctification, a separation. Those who were with Korah died, and those who had separated themselves from him lived.

Paul wrote:

> *Be ye not unequally yoked together with unbeliev-ers: for what fellowship hath righteousness with unrighteousness? and what communion hath light with darkness?*   2 Corinthians 6:14

This verse is not just for marriage relationships. It is much more than that. We are not to be entangled with unbelievers. To the contrary, we are to get out from among them, be separate, and not touch unclean things.

Another scriptures says, *"Depart"*:

> *And, let every one that nameth the name of Christ depart from iniquity.*   2 Timothy 2:19

What does it mean to depart? At an airport, you hear about departures and arrivals. If you are leaving Chicago to go to Hawaii to lie on the beach, and you go to arrivals instead of departures, you will never reach your destination. There is a point of arrival and there's a point of departure. Justification is a point of departure. Get out!

A Call to Consecration

Sanctification simply means to deny yourself, take up your cross, and follow Jesus. How do you deny yourself? The key is being dead in Christ. What can a dead man do? Nothing. What can a dead man say? Nothing. Where can a dead man go? Nowhere. That's why the Bible says:

> *Likewise reckon ye also yourselves to be dead indeed unto sin, but alive unto God through Jesus Christ our Lord.*   Romans 6:11

To the Galatians, Paul wrote:

> *I am crucified with Christ: nevertheless I live; yet not I, but Christ liveth in me: and the life which I now live in the flesh I live by the faith of the Son of God, who loved me, and gave himself for me.*
>   Galatians 2:20

If you've ever been to a funeral you know that the body in the casket doesn't move. It doesn't talk. If you say something, it doesn't react. That person is dead.

You can curse them and their eyebrow won't move. You say good things about them, and they won't react.

When you're dead, you have no more rights. I have never known of a dead person going to court to claim their rights. They have none. When you sanctify yourself, you lose all personal rights. That's why Paul could write:

But what things were gain to me, those I counted loss for Christ. Yea doubtless, and I count all things but loss for the excellency of the knowledge of Christ Jesus my Lord: for whom I have suffered the loss of all things, and do count them but dung, that I may win Christ, and be found in him, not having mine own righteousness, which is of the law, but that which is through the faith of Christ, the righteousness which is of God by faith.

Philippians 3:7-9

This is a call to a life of separation. Let this year be a year of spiritual growth and maturing in God. It can only happen as you concentrate your efforts on things that can build up your spirit more than things that can appease and bring comfort to your flesh.

The greater the price to be paid, the richer the reward will be. If you want junk, go to a garage sale or a thrift store. Keep in mind that you are buying things others no longer want. You will be very lucky if you find something worthwhile. If you want some-thing of quality, go to Marshall Fields or Lord and Taylor. You will get what you are willing to pay for. If you are only willing to spend twenty-five cents, you will get twenty-five cents worth. If you lose that item, it won't break your heart. But if it cost you five hundred dollars, you would cry a bucket of tears. That loss is painful.

Your life is worth a lot more than a few thou-sand dollars. The true value of it is more than all the riches of this world. God has invested in your soul the greatest treasure of Heaven, His Son, Jesus Christ. Let us show our appreciation by living a life of consecration.

Spend more time in God's Word. Spend more time in fellowship with His people in church. Spend more time in prayer. Spend more time worshiping and praising God rather than murmuring and com-plaining. Spend more time counting your blessings rather than counting your problems. Spend more time looking up rather than looking down. Spend your time progressing, going forward, rather than regressing and going backward.

Determine in your heart today that by the help of God you will do exactly what is required of you so that you will receive everything that God has for you. You need to determine that in your heart.

Have you tasted the goodness of the Lord? If so, how can you be satisfied with anything else? Are you willing to pay the price to receive everything that God has prepared for you? This is a call to consecration.

CHAPTER 4

A CALL TO CONSECRATION: PART 4

Thy word is a lamp unto my feet, and a light unto
my path. I have sworn, and I will perform it, that
I will keep thy righteous judgments.

Psalm 119:105-106

Many years ago I read an article saying that the famous performer, Madonna, planned to bring up her baby knowing the Bible. That would have been great, but I was praying that she would get saved. How could an ungodly person who had never taken time for the Lord raise a child on the Bible. Something about that didn't add up. Madonna needed to start following the Bible herself, and we do too.

Once you start opening your heart to the Word of God and reading it with an open heart, it will penetrate your spirit. And when God gets hold of your heart, anything can happen.

I knew a man who read the Bible just so he would be able to argue with certain Christians. He was especially interested in Proverbs and Ecclesiastes. His motive, of course, was wrong, but as he searched the Scriptures, God got hold of his spirit, and he got saved. Then, instead of arguing with believers, he started helping them, supporting them, and preaching the Word of God himself.

When you open your heart to the Word of God, something happens to you. A conviction takes place, and when such a conviction comes, it penetrates. It's like a nail being hammered into your heart. You are forced to make one of two decisions. Either you will decide to yield to the Word of God or you will resist the dealings of the Lord.

The Spirit of God uses the Word to speak to the hearts of men, and His Word will never return void or unfulfilled. That Word has power to change situations.

He sent his word, and healed them, and delivered them from their destructions.   Psalm 107:20

There's power in the Word of God, and I encourage all those who desire to consecrate themselves to God to take more time reading His Word. Personally I like to read through the Bible twice a year. I don't always start with Genesis. Sometimes I start in the New Testament. If God has made His Word available to us, how can we not take advantage of it?

Educate yourself in the Word of God. Digest it. Meditate on it. Plant it in your heart. This is not to say that you will understand everything you're reading. There are many mysteries in God's Word. Read it anyway because it can get into your heart, mind, and spirit. Then, when you need it, the Spirit of God can quicken it to your spirit, and it will become a blessing to you.

Once you begin to get the overall picture of the Bible, then go deeper. Let God reveal it to you layer upon layer. You will never run out of fresh manna.

It is sad to me that people who have been saved for ten, twenty, or even thirty years know so little of God's Word. That ought not to be. Many have never read the Bible from cover to cover. What do they expect? If we haven't laid proper foundations, what can we expect God to do?

I know that justification, sanctification, and consecration are big-sounding words, but their meaning is not complicated or hard to understand. What is the relationship of sanctification to our consecration? Again, sanctification means being set apart or made holy. Other words might be godly, righteous, pure, clean.

Paul wrote to the Thessalonians:

Furthermore then we beseech you, brethren, and exhort you by the Lord Jesus, that as ye have received of us how ye ought to walk and to please God, so ye would abound more and more. For ye know what commandments we gave you by the Lord Jesus. For this is the will of God, even your sanctification, that ye should abstain from fornication: that every one of you should know how to possess his vessel in sanctification and honour.

1 Thessalonians 4:1-4

This is *"how ye ought to walk."* Paul was not talking about physical exercise; he was talking about how we should live life. He is describing a style of living, how you conduct yourself, how you behave. It relates to the places you go, the things you do, the things you say. That's all part of the Christian walk.

As Christians, we need to walk straight. The way we conduct ourselves, our attitude, our character, our disposition in life, must reflect Christ. We must walk in a way that is pleasing to Him:

A Call to Consecration

That ye might walk worthy of the Lord unto all pleasing, being fruitful in every good work, and increasing in the knowledge of God; strengthened with all might, according to his glorious power, unto all patience and longsuffering with joyfulness; giving thanks unto the Father, which hath made us meet to be partakers of the inheritance of the saints in light.   Colossians 1:10-12

How do we please God? By obeying Him, by trusting Him, and by relying on Him. Our faith pleases God:

But without faith it is impossible to please him: for he that cometh to God must believe that he is, and that he is a rewarder of them that diligently seek him.   Hebrews 11:6

Our worship pleases God. Our prayers please God. Our keeping of the commandments pleases God. Loving Him with all our hearts, mind, soul, and spirit pleases God. Loving others as He loves us pleases God. Tithing pleases God. Living a sanctified life pleases God.

Being sanctified simply refers to the way you live. As a believer you are set apart to become more like Jesus.

There is, of course, a process required for becoming like Him. That's where many fall back. Becoming like Jesus is easy enough to say, but how do you actually accomplish it?

It requires knowing what God expects of you and then being willing to obey Him. It requires study and meditation and waiting on the Spirit, and it requires humility, dying to the flesh, dying to the common appetites of man. And this all depends on having an intimate relationship with God.

That's the bottom line. That's where it all starts and ends. If there is no proper relationship, how could we possibly please God? If the relationship is right, everything else will fall in line.

The only way you can please your wife or husband is to have a solid and lasting relationship. And how do you establish such a relationship? It takes all of the elements I have already mentioned.

After all Peter had seen, why would he deny the Lord? The passage says that he was following *"afar off"*:

> *But Peter followed him afar off unto the high priest's palace, and went in, and sat with the servants, to see the end.*　　Matthew 26:58

A Call to Consecration

Peter knew the Lord, but his relationship with the Lord at this moment was distant. You can attend church your whole life and still have no relationship with God. You can give tithes and offering and even your body to be offered as a sacrifice and still have no relationship with God. You can even memorize scriptures, and it doesn't mean that you have a relationship with God. All of these things are important and necessary for us in our process of growth, but alone they don't mean that you are really serving the Lord. Jesus said:

> *Not every one that saith unto me, Lord, Lord, shall enter into the kingdom of heaven; but he that doeth the will of my Father which is in heaven.*
>
> Matthew 7:21

What is the will of the Father? Let's see it from His Word:

> *Be ye not unequally yoked together with unbelievers: for what fellowship hath righteousness with unrighteousness? and what communion hath light with darkness?*   2 Corinthians 6:14

97

God is not calling you to cut off all ties with sinners because we are to be the light of the world. But we cannot be yoked with them. This doesn't mean that you can't talk to unbelievers or go shopping with unbelievers. It means that we are not to be one with them in thinking or in lifestyle. We are not to be in harmony with their activities. We can relate to them and testify to them, but we must not be partakers of the kind of life they are living.

Jesus sat down with sinners. As a matter of fact, the Pharisees and the Sadducees were angry that He was eating with publicans and sinners, but He did not compromise, and He did not yoke Himself with them, to do what they were doing. His life, in the midst of sinners, made the difference for them. He was able to show them the Light, to show them the Truth of what the Word of God teaches. We, like Him, need sanctification.

Sanctification is a setting apart. We must make the decision to separate ourselves from everything that is ungodly, from everything that is not of God. We must disassociate ourselves from anything that would contaminate us and make us impure.

And what concord hath Christ with Belial? or what part hath he that believeth with an infidel?

A Call to Consecration

And what agreement hath the temple of God with idols? for ye are the temple of the living God; as God hath said, I will dwell in them, and walk in them; and I will be their God, and they shall be my people. Wherefore come out from among them, and be ye separate, saith the Lord, and touch not the unclean thing; and I will receive you. And will be a Father unto you, and ye shall be my sons and daughters, saith the Lord Almighty.

2 Corinthians 6:15-18

Who was Belial? He was the god of this world. If you are a Christian and you're friend is not a Christian, there is already a line drawn as far as values are concerned. If you're a true Christian and a true follower of Jesus Christ and you are living a life of consecration, those who are ungodly will know, without you having to preach to them, that you are a follower of Jesus Christ. Just the fact that you are not doing what they're doing speaks volumes.

Some may wonder why we don't drink, we don't smoke, and we don't do drugs. I don't need all of that to be a man. Others see the difference.

I can fellowship with the unsaved only to a certain degree. If my fellowship leads me to become unequally yoked with them to the point that I'm doing exactly what they're doing, then I would be destroying my testimony and putting my relationship with God in danger. If we play around with sin too long, we just might see our salvation fly out the window.

There is no agreement between darkness and light. The one expels the other. Our light makes all the difference. Darkness is overpowered by light.

When you associate with non-believers, and they are in darkness, if you are not shining your light, not sanctifying yourself, but are doing exactly what they're doing, then you are sending those people to destruction, and you will be responsible for them. Look again at those last few verses:

Ye are the temple of the living God; as God hath said, I will dwell in them, and walk in them; and I will be their God, and they shall be my people. Wherefore come out from among them, and be ye separate, saith the Lord, and touch not the unclean thing; and I will receive you. And will be a Father unto you, and ye shall be my sons and daughters, saith the Lord Almighty.

2 Corinthians 6:16-18

A Call to Consecration

What beautiful words! Underline that verse in your Bible and register it clearly in your mind. *"What agreement?"* There can be none.

We are the temple of the Holy Spirit. The Spirit of God does not dwell in a temple made of hands. A church building is not the real house of God. Our bodies are His house. A church is not the only place of worship. My body must be a place of worship and a house of prayer. This body is the dwelling place, the residence, of God Almighty. What a privilege! That's why there can be no agreement with darkness, no union, no fellowship between God's people and Satan.

Let me be blunt. Idol worship is not just bowing down before graven images and lighting candles for them. An idol is anything that is more important to you than God. That could be something as simple as food. It could be owning material things. It could be idolizing your wife or husband or a child. Anything that is more important to you than God is your idol.

Baseball can become an idol. Basketball can become an idol. Football and the Superbowl can (and does) become an idol. Anything that you devote more time and energy into becomes your god.

A ministry can become a god. The church itself can become a god. God will not share His glory with anyone or anything.

Would a loving husband want to share his wife with someone else? Never! It's done in the world, but only by those with a reprobate mind. No loving spouse would think of it, and God will not share His glory with another.

As we have seen, God said in 2 Corinthians 6:16, *"I will dwell in them, and walk in them; and I will be their God, and they shall be my people."* Paul also wrote:

> *For in him we live, and move, and have our being.* Acts 17:28

> *To whom God would make known what is the riches of the glory of this mystery among the Gentiles; which is Christ in you, the hope of glory.*
> Colossians 1:27

John wrote to the churches:

> *Ye are of God, little children, and have overcome them: because greater is he that is in you, than he that is in the world.* 1 John 4:4

A Call to Consecration

"He … is in you." What more could we ask? He lives in us and works through us. He, therefore, has promised to direct our path, guiding us in all things. He brightens our path and makes all the crooked ways straight. He opens to us doors that no one else can open, and when we go through them, He walks with us. Because God is with us, we can successfully face any foe. Even if all the legions of Hell rise up against us, we have nothing to fear.

When we sanctify ourselves, consecrating our lives to God, we are preparing our vessel to become His dwelling place so that He can live in us, move in us, walk with us, and talk with us. He can also demonstrate His power in and through our lives.

What a beautiful thing! The Creator of Heaven and Earth lives in you. God is not against you. He is on your side. He said, *"I will be their God, and they shall be my people."* That's not me speaking but God Himself.

This is not the words of some commentary or of a Bible scholar. These are God's words, the Omnipotent (the All-Powerful), the Omniscient (the All-Knowing), the Omnipresent (the Everywhere Present). Our God is unmovable, unchangeable, and infinite. He has no limitations, and He has said that

He will be everything that He is in you when He becomes the only God for you.

When you consecrate your life, sanctifying it to God, you are telling Him, "Be my God. Be everything that You are in and through me."

There's a song that says:

If you know the Lord,
You need nobody else,
To see you through
The darkest night.
You can walk alone,
You only need the Lord
To keep you on the road
Marked right.
Take time to pray, every day;
And when you're heading home,
He'll show you the way.
If you know the Lord,
You need nobody else,
To see the Light,
God's wonderful light.[1]

---

1. Songwriter: S Bickley "Bix" Reichner

A Call to Consecration

God is saying to you today: everything that He is is exactly what He will be in you. He will be your God. He is the God of Abraham (a God of covenant), the God of Isaac (a God of promise), the God of Jacob (a God of blessing). He will be a God to all those who sanctify themselves, consecrate themselves to live for Him a life of total separation.

"I will be their God." Not perhaps or maybe, but *"I will!"* He will be everything to us. Not only will He be out God, but we shall be His people.

One day I and some ministry companions were in the airport in India and saw a black lady from Africa. She was touring. I said to Nate, one of my companions, "There's a sister over there."

"Yeah," he said, "she's a sister."

We went and sat down close to the lady and began to converse, and sure enough, she was a believer. God's people are so unique that you can spot them from a distance. God called us *"a chosen generation, a royal priesthood, an holy nation, a peculiar people"*:

> *But ye are a chosen generation, a royal priesthood, an holy nation, a peculiar people; that ye should*

*shew forth the praises of him who hath called you
out of darkness into his marvellous light.*

1 Peter 2:9

We are God's people. Think about that. What does it mean to be the people of God, the sheep of His pasture. If we were talking about your family, you would do everything within your power to make that family blessed. If you are a normal parent, you would never allow your children to go hungry. If they were threatened, you would stand and fight for their safety, security, and protection. How much more the God of the Universe?

Since we are His family, we are under His covering. He will protect us. He will fight for us. He will defend us. He will supply our needs. He will be everything we need in life, Jehovah-Jireh, El Shaddai, the God of Plenty. He will do this because we are His people.

We are not just Americans, not just Africans, not just Filipinos, not just Orientals, and not just Europeans. We are people of God. We are His holy nation, His peculiar people. Never forget it: we are His dwelling place. He walks in us and through us. He is our God, and we are His people.

A Call to Consecration

"Wherefore come out from among them." Because of this, separate yourself from the unbelieving and live the peculiar life of the believer."

Who is the *"them"* in this phrase? Those who are not the people of God, those who are not His dwelling place, those who do not love Him or desire to follow Him. Get out from among them.

What does it mean to get out? It means to separate from them. Let them go.

> *And ye be separate, saith the Lord. And touch not the unclean thing.*

It is not enough just to separate yourself from the unbelieving. You have to take it a step further and not touch *"the unclean thing."*

Galatians 5 lists the fruits of the flesh:

> *Now the works of the flesh are manifest, which are these; Adultery, fornication, uncleanness, lasciviousness, Idolatry, witchcraft, hatred, variance, emulations, wrath, strife, seditions, heresies, Envyings, murders, drunkenness, revellings, and such like: of the which I tell you before, as I have*

also told you in time past, that they which do such things shall not inherit the kingdom of God.
Galatians 5:19-21

One day, many years ago, I met a friend at a birthday party. I approached him and extended my hand to shake with him and greet him, but he said, "Go away! Go, leave me alone," and he kept backing up.

I'm not sure what his problem was that day, but I said, "Okay, God bless you," and I turned and went the other way. As you can imagine, that experience left me with a feeling of rejection. How would you feel if your spouse said to you, "I don't love me anymore. Please release me and let me go?" That would crush you.

What a feeling of ecstasy comes to you when the response is, "I love you!" That gives you a sense of worth, a sense of security, a sense of belonging. You feel that you are important. God said, *"I will receive you."*

Think of the expression of a young child when Mama or Papa has just come back from somewhere and is walking into the house. That child comes running, and those parents extend a warm embrace.

Think of the prodigal son. After all that he had done, he decided to return to his father, even if it meant being a humble servant. But the father received him with open arms, loving him, caring for him, and restoring him to his position. God said, *"I will receive you."*

If someone knocks on your door and you welcome them in and entertain them, you give that person a wonderful feeling. If you were to open the door and say, "I don't want to talk with you; go away," how would they feel? You have just killed that person. Maybe they were not an angel, not a prophet, and not a pastor, but you devastated them.

God said, *"I will receive you."* He welcomes you into His presence. He welcomes you into His anointing. He welcomes you into His glory. He receives you.

It is not a denomination saying that, it's not a church, and it's not an association. It is God Himself and He is saying, *"I will receive you."* You are important to Him. You are precious to Him. He will not turn His back on you.

John wrote:

> *Behold, what manner of love the Father hath bestowed upon us, that we should be called the sons of God.*   1 John 3:1

What a powerful verse! God said, *"I will receive you."*

That 18th verse of 2 Corinthians 6 is just as powerful:

And [I] will be a Father unto you, and ye shall be my sons and daughters, saith the Lord Almighty.

"I will be a Father unto you." Underline that in your Bible. Write it down. Make a poster of it. Read it often. *"I will be a Father unto you."*

Jesus said we should pray, *"Our Father, which art in heaven."* Why? Because God said, *"I will be a Father unto you."* What does a father do? He provides. He comforts. He protects. He defends. He disciplines. He corrects. He chastises. He rebukes. He admonishes. He encourages. *"I will be a father unto you."*

I lost my dad when I was seven years old. I had never enjoyed being around him as I was growing up because he was always sick. He died very young. I never really felt the love of an earthly father. He was always in the hospital or lying in bed at home. We would sometimes gather around his bed, and we could touch him, but that's about as far as it went. There was no real intimate relationship.

A Call to Consecration

When I got saved, my Saviour was not only my Redeemer; He also became my Father. He loved me, accepted me the way I was, and was proud of me. He helped me to become what I should be in Him. It was only when I got saved that I felt what a father's love could be. He didn't come to condemn me, but to save me. He was not acting like a judge. He was a loving heavenly Father.

And He is *your* Father too. You don't need to turn to anyone else. You don't need to be running here and there. Just come to the Father. Jesus taught:

> *If ye then, being evil, know how to give good gifts unto your children: how much more shall your heavenly Father give the Holy Spirit to them that ask him?*   Luke 11:13

The verses leading up to that are important. Let's see them in Matthew:

> *What man is there of you, whom if his son ask bread, will he give him a stone? Or if he ask a fish, will he give him a serpent? If ye then, being evil, know how to give good gifts unto your children,*

how much more shall your Father which is in heaven give good things to them that ask him?

Matthew 7:9-11

Paul wrote to the Romans:

He that spared not his own Son, but delivered him up for us all, how shall he not with him also freely give us all things? Romans 8:32

Yes, He is our Father. You are the apple of His eye. If every Christian could just grasp these truths, we would quickly end our troubles with the Christian walk. We are destined to be overcomers in every way. We are to live triumphantly, abounding in the blessings of God and increasing in the knowledge of the Lord. We were not destined to run and hide when opposition arises. God is with us. He is our God, and we are His people. Therefore we have nothing to fear.

Let us sanctify ourselves. Let us surrender our lives to God totally and allow the promises of the Scriptures to become a reality in us. This is a call to consecration.

CHAPTER 5

A CALL TO CONSECRATION,:PART 5

Our bodies are made of clay, yet we have the treasure of the Good News in them. This shows that the superior power of this treasure belongs to God and doesn't come from us.

2 Corinthians 4:7, NOG

When you look in a mirror, say to the person you see, "There is gold inside that clay." Yes, Jesus dwells in there, and with Him, the power of God and the glory of God. Your flesh may still have limitations, flaws, shortcomings, and weaknesses, but inside, you are being purified. The Holy Spirit is developing pure gold in you.

Inside of that clay is the image of God. The Holy Spirit has a hammer and chisel and He is working to remove the covering so that the glory of the image of Christ in you can be revealed in this sinful world. What a revelation!

When you look at yourself, don't consider all that the devil is doing. See yourself as God sees you.

You are not defeated in the eyes of God; you are victorious. You are not poor in the eyes of God; you are rich in His grace and mercy. You are a partaker of His blessings. We need to rearrange our thinking and our mental attitude. We are children of God. We are the people of God, and we are being purified for His glory.

In order to purify you, God allows you to experience stressful situations. He allows trials and tribulations to come your way. He wants you to come out of your cocoon, spread your wings, and take flight.

A mother eagle is very wise. She knows when it's time for her little eaglets to start learning to fly, and what she does is ingenious. Little by little, she begins to remove the softer elements of the nest. Those eaglets are too comfortable. Left alone, they will stay right where they are. They are waiting for Mama to keep feeding them, but Mama has other ideas. She wants to get them out of the nest.

As she slowly removes the cushioning, what remains starts sticking them and they start thinking about getting out of there. They start stretching their wings. When the nest gets uncomfortable enough, they will start moving out and learning to fly.

A Call to Consecration

God wants us to move out of our comfort zone. What feels harsh to us is the Spirit of God moving and working to get us to where we need to be. We need to fly. We were created to fly.

What does that have to do with a call to consecration? Everything. Let's continue.

We covered justification that brings us into a definite relationship with God. Justification brings forgiveness. Justification brings the cleansing of our sin. Justification opens the door and plants us firmly in the Kingdom of God. Justification acquits us from every guilt because Christ took our blame and our shame.

We also covered sanctification. That is the process of molding us and shaping us to become more like Christ. If you really want to become more like Him, there will be pressure applied to you. When you want to bake a cake or some bread, you need to mix the dough. You put some pressure on it. Then you let it rise. And, finally, you put it into the oven.

We don't like to be in the oven, but if we want to grow in God, if we want to become more like Jesus, if we want to become more like the image of Christ, we need to be put into a place where we can be purified, where we can be cleansed.

The hammer and chisel are in the hands of the Spirit and He is working to remove all that is covering the image inside the clay. Michael Angelo carved his famous sculpture of David. He could visualize that image inside the rock and said it had always been there. He just needed to release it.

The image of Christ is always there inside of this clay. We just need to allow the Holy Spirit to remove anything and everything that obscures it. Sometimes the Spirit uses your pastor, sometimes your spouse, your children, your friends, or other members of the Body of Christ to remove some of the excess and the rough edges of life so that the divine image will come forth.

When the Spirit of God is finished with us, we will shine with the beauty of Jesus from the inside out. Christ is in us, and people need to see Him. Let all the windows of your life be open so that Christ can be revealed to other people around you.

Sanctification is a process. It is instant in one sense. When Christ comes into your life, you instantly change. You are a new creature in Christ. However, you are not yet a mature believer in any sense of the word. You are just a babe, and you have a lot to learn. In that sense, sanctification is a progressive work.

A Call to Consecration

Babies are righteous, but they are far from perfect. They have a lot of growing to do, and the Christian life is the same. When you're saved, you have new life, but you don't know much yet.

Instantly you are righteous, and you don't have to work for that. You don't have to do anything but believe. There's nothing you *can* do. Jesus did it all for you.

You have been forgiven of all past sins and passed from death unto life. That is all instantaneousness. But that was just like a seed being planted. Now begins the continuous process of maturing, and with it, the continuous process of sanctification.

When a husband and wife are intimate sexually, something happens instantly. An egg and a sperm meet, and a new life is planted in the wife's womb. She is now pregnant, but the actual birth takes time. There is a process of growth and development that must play out. In time, a baby is born. That's how sanctification works too.

The last process we want to consider in this book is glorification. These words all sound alike: *justification, sanctification,* and *glorification*. It sounds easy, but it's not. It requires the crucifixion of the flesh. Your flesh needs to die so that you can experience God's glory.

Ray Llarena

*Likewise reckon ye also yourselves to be dead in-
deed unto sin, but alive unto God through Jesus
Christ our Lord.*   Romans 6:11

"Dead unto sin, but alive unto God." The appetites
and the lusts of the flesh must be put under the
control of the Holy Spirit. Walking in the flesh must
come to an end, and we must start walking in the
Spirit. Carnality must be subdued, and we must
learn to be led by the Spirit.

There is a definite price to pay. You cannot enter into the fullness of God's blessing until you
have determined to have your own Garden of
Gethsemane experience. You will never become
what God intended you to be and never receive
everything that God has for you until you determine within your heart that you are willing to go
to Gethsemane.

It is not enough just to enter the garden gates. You
must move into the inner part of the Garden, find a
rock where you can pray, and sweat as it were drops
of blood. That's the process of sanctification. We die
daily to the things of this world:

I die daily.   1 Corinthians 15:31

What did Paul mean by this? He had to die to the flesh, and the more we die to the flesh, the more alive we become in the Spirit.

Christ didn't really die on Calvary. He died in Gethsemane. He died when He prayed those fateful words:

Father, if thou be willing, remove this cup from me: nevertheless not my will, but thine, be done.

Luke 22:42

In that moment, Jesus died, and our salvation was complete, and it happened in Gethsemane. In that moment, the battle was won. When Jesus said yes to the will of the Father, the battle ended, the war was finished, and the enemy was conquered. As Jesus submitted Himself to the purpose and the plan and program of His Father and removed Himself from His own desires and plans, He died right then and there.

Gethsemane cannot be avoided or escaped by those who desire to grow and mature in God. There is no other way. You cannot escape it. You must go through it.

The beautiful thing about it is this: after Gethsemane, you can endure Calvary. You can endure carrying your cross because you died in Gethsemane. The reason we keep coming down off the cross is that Gethsemane has not yet been settled in our hearts. *"Thy will be done"* must become our prayer too. There is no other way.

Sanctification is putting your life in the will of God and letting Him consume you. You are no longer your own; you are His. You have finally come to the absolute recognition of His total Lordship, control, and sovereignty over your life. You have come to a place where you acknowledge who He is, and you have submitted your life completely to Him.

One day God spoke to the prophet Jeremiah to go to a potter's house and observe what was being done there. He obeyed and saw that the clay was being shaped, first through the application of water and then through the pressure of the potter's hands. When any imperfection was found in a vessel, the potter started over. He shaped the clay again and again until it finally became a vessel fit for the master's use. That's the process we're going through.

What is glorification? It is the consummation of our salvation. Justification is the beginning of our salvation, sanctification is the progress and the on-going growth of our salvation, of our relationship with Jesus Christ, and glorification is the consummation of our salvation. It is the final destination and arrival point of our spiritual journey. Paul wrote:

> *That I may know him, and the power of his resurrection, and the fellowship of his sufferings, being made conformable unto his death; if by any means I might attain unto the resurrection of the dead. Not as though I had already attained, either were already perfect: but I follow after, if that I may apprehend that for which also I am apprehended of Christ Jesus. Brethren, I count not myself to have apprehended: but this one thing I do, forgetting those things which are behind, and reaching forth unto those things which are before, I press toward the mark for the prize of the high calling of God in Christ Jesus.* Philippians 3:10-14

Forgetting the things which are behind and reaching forth for the things which are before is a key to achieving glorification. It involves pressing toward the mark of the prize of the high calling of God in Christ Jesus. Glorification is our point of arrival. It is our point of completion.

As Jesus was hanging on the cross, He said, *"It is finished."* What did He mean by that? He had done the job. At the time of our glorification, we will also say, "It's completed. I have arrived. I am now complete in Him."

Glorification is the place where we are finally transformed completely into the image of Christ. We will have arrived to perfection, and there will be nothing more that needs to be changed in us, nothing more to be altered. The work is completely done. When this happens, you will no longer be here, subject to earth's atmosphere, time, space, and the elements. You will no longer be controlled by this life. You will have passed on to the highest level of life. That's what glorification is all about.

And be not conformed to this world: but be ye transformed by the renewing of your mind, that ye may prove what is that good, and acceptable, and perfect, will of God. Romans 12:2

Don't be conformed; be transformed. How? By the renewing of your mind. That's real change. No wonder the Bible tells us:

A Call to Consecration

Precious in the sight of the LORD is the death of his saints. Psalm 116:15

As a believer takes his or her last breath here on earth, they enter into God's glory. In the process, they become glorified and enter into an incorruptible and endless life by being ushered into the very presence of God.

But some man will say, How are the dead raised up? and with what body do they come? Thou fool, that which thou sowest is not quickened, except it die: and that which thou sowest, thou sowest not that body that shall be, but bare grain, it may chance of wheat, or of some other grain: but God giveth it a body as it hath pleased him, and to every seed his own body. 1 Corinthians 15:35-38

Jesus said:

Verily, verily, I say unto you, Except a corn of wheat fall into the ground and die, it abideth alone: but if it die, it bringeth forth much fruit.
John 12:24

There is life in a kernel of corn. It has the potential to become life-giving, to multiply and become something much grander. But despite that potential, if that seed is not planted in the ground, it will not produce. When it's planted, it dies, and out of that death springs new life and a great harvest.

When you plant one kernel of corn, you can harvest a complete stock of corn with one or two ears of corn on it, and each ear of corn bears more than 600 kernels. This means that one single kernel planted produces from 600 to 1,200 kernels, some more.

Paul continued in 1 Corinthians 15:

> *All flesh is not the same flesh: but there is one kind of flesh of men, another flesh of beasts, another of fishes, and another of birds. There are also celestial bodies, and bodies terrestrial: but the glory of the celestial is one, and the glory of the terrestrial is another. There is one glory of the sun, and another glory of the moon, and another glory of the stars: for one star differeth from another star in glory. So also is the resurrection of the dead. It is sown in corruption; it is raised in incorruption: it is sown in dishonour; it is raised in glory: it is sown in*

weakness; it is raised in power: it is sown a natural body; it is raised a spiritual body.
There is a natural body and there is a spiritual body.   1 Corinthians 15:39-44

The rest of the chapter is worth reading as well:

And so it is written, The first man Adam was made a living soul; the last Adam was made a quickening spirit. Howbeit that was not first which is spiritual, but that which is natural; and afterward that which is spiritual. The first man is of the earth, earthy; the second man is the Lord from heaven. As is the earthy, such are they also that are earthy: and as is the heavenly, such are they also that are heavenly. And as we have borne the image of the earthy, we shall also bear the image of the heavenly.
Now this I say, brethren, that flesh and blood cannot inherit the kingdom of God; neither doth corruption inherit incorruption. Behold, I shew you a mystery; We shall not all sleep, but we shall all be changed, in a moment, in the twinkling of an eye, at the last trump: for the trumpet shall sound, and the dead shall be raised incorruptible,

and we shall be changed. For this corruptible must put on incorruption, and this mortal must put on immortality. So when this corruptible shall have put on incorruption, and this mortal shall have put on immortality, then shall be brought to pass the saying that is written, Death is swallowed up in victory.

O death, where is thy sting?
O grave, where is thy victory?

The sting of death is sin; and the strength of sin is the law. But thanks be to God, which giveth us the victory through our Lord Jesus Christ.
Therefore, my beloved brethren, be ye stedfast, unmoveable, always abounding in the work of the Lord, forasmuch as ye know that your labour is not in vain in the Lord. 1 Corinthians 15:45-56

Basically, Paul was saying that we were born into this earth with an earthly body, and that body goes through a process of growth. It arrives at the pinnacle of its growth and then begins to decay. If you have been suffering some pain and see physical changes and don't like what you see, those changes that are taking place in the physical realm are preparing us for the incorruptible. The corruptible and the incorruptible cannot mix. The Bible tells us that new wine cannot be put into old wineskins.

There is a life that cannot decay, cannot be corrupted, and will never die. But the physical body is subject to death. All of this happens over time. Your hair changes color. Wrinkles appear on your face. Your steps slow. It is all part of the aging process. It means that your body has arrived at the pinnacle of its growth and is now beginning to decline. But the beauty of it all is that even as the natural life is declining, the spiritual life is taking greater control. At least that should be the case.

The more the natural declines the more control your spirit man can take. It will not be the flesh transforming the flesh. It will be the spirit that transforms the flesh.

The apostle Paul is showing us that there is a process that must take place before we can arrive at an incorruptible state. There is a physical process of change, and there is nothing much we can do about that. It will happen.

Just a few years ago, you were a teenager. Now, suddenly, you're seventy years old, and your strength is not what it was when you were a teenager. Your hearing sometimes is not as good. But the more our natural hearing becomes dulled, the more our spiritual hearing should become sensitive. As you are becoming forgetful in the natural, the spirit man should become more alert inside of you. As the natural is starting to fade, the spiritual man should be becoming more and more in control. This transition should continue until we have arrived at our final destination when we become like Jesus.

Paul wrote:

For now we see through a glass, darkly; but then face to face: now I know in part; but then shall I know even as also I am known.

1 Corinthians 13:12

John wrote:

Beloved, now are we the sons of God, and it doth not yet appear what we shall be: but we know that, when he shall appear, we shall be like him; for we shall see him as he is.　　　1 John 3:2

A Call to Consecration

"It doth not yet appear." What we do know is that we will be like Him. After all the struggles are past and He has purified us, we will see Him and be like Him. What more could we ask for?

Again, Paul wrote:

We having the same spirit of faith, according as it is written, I believed, and therefore have I spoken; we also believe, and therefore speak; knowing that he which raised up the Lord Jesus shall raise up us also by Jesus, and shall present us with you.

2 Corinthians 4:13-14

What does it mean? God was bringing Paul to a place where he could be presented. He went on:

For all things are for your sakes, that the abundant grace might through the thanksgiving of many redound to the glory of God. For which cause we faint not; but though our outward man perish, yet the inward man is renewed day by day.

2 Corinthians 4:15-16

Paul was talking about the experiences of life—persecution, hunger, imprisonment, beatings. All of these happened in his life after he became born again. After he surrendered his life to God, he experienced terrible things. At one point, he had to be lowered down the wall of the city in a basket because people were after him. He was shipwrecked and bitten by a snake.

And Paul suffered the same physical deterioration we all do. *"Though our outward man perish ..."* His physical body was groaning, aching, being disturbed, inconvenienced, tormented, tortured. His outward man was perishing. It was agonizing, going through pain, going through hardship, going through suffering. *"Yet,"* he said triumphantly, *"the inward man is renewed day by day."* That is glorification.

The suffering, the trials, the agony, the hardship, the temptations, and the persecutions are all to prepare us for the glory that is coming.

> *For our light affliction, which is but for a moment, worketh for us a far more exceeding and eternal weight of glory.*   2 Corinthians 4:17

"Our light affliction ..." It is bearable, endurable, acceptable because we know that it is leading us to something so wonderful. Jesus said:

A Call to Consecration

Take my yoke upon you, and learn of me; for I am meek and lowly in heart: and ye shall find rest unto your souls. For my yoke is easy, and my burden is light. Matthew 11:29-30

"My burden is light." It's not heavy. It's not unreasonable. It is bearable, endurable, light. *"Our light affliction"* speaks of sufferings, trials, hardships, headaches, you name it, whatever is attacking this physical body of ours. But, Paul said, it is *"but for a moment."* It's temporary. It's not permanent. It's just for a moment. The trials, the sufferings, the hardships, the inconveniences, the difficulties are all just for a moment. The good news is that it's all working *"for us a far more exceeding and eternal weight of glory."* Our glorification will be far greater than any suffering we might have to go through here.

Paul said:

I have fought a good fight, I have finished my course, I have kept the faith: henceforth there is laid up for me a crown of righteousness, which the Lord, the righteous judge, shall give me at that day: and not to me only, but unto all them also that love his appearing. 2 Timothy 4:7-8

Ray Llarena

It's worth the fight. The prize for finishing the race and keeping the faith will make it worth it all. What awaits us now is a crown of righteousness. That's much better than any trophy this world has to offer. It means eternal life.

Those who compete in the Olympics are tenacious. They fight their way to the finish line, and to get there they put themselves under a strict regime of self-control, subjection to strict rules of diet, exercise, and rest. Anything and everything that might hinder them from success and victory is set aside, and all to receive a corruptible reward. How much more should put our time and energy into receiving that which is incorruptible, that which can never be destroyed! Our reward cannot be eaten by moths or destroyed by fire, and it cannot rust away. It will never be taken from us.

Peter wrote:

Blessed be the God and Father of our Lord Jesus Christ, which according to his abundant mercy hath begotten us again unto a lively hope by the resurrection of Jesus Christ from the dead, to an inheritance incorruptible, and undefiled, and that fadeth not away, reserved in heaven for you, who

132

are kept by the power of God through faith unto
salvation ready to be revealed in the last time.

1 Peter 1:3-5

We can look up because the time of our glorification is drawing near. There is a point of arrival at perfection. We cannot look to this world and all the things that are happening in it. We must have a different attitude. When we look at the world, we remember that song again:

This world is not my home.
I'm just a-passing through.
My treasures are laid up
Somewhere beyond the blue

The angels beckon me
From Heaven's open door
And I can't feel at home
In this world anymore.[1]

Yes, we're just passing through. It's all just for a moment. It's quickly passing. Paul concluded:

_____
1. Songwriter: Jim Reeves

We look not at the things which are seen, but at the things which are not seen: for the things which are seen are temporal; but the things which are not seen are eternal. 2 Corinthians 4:18

That's why he could say:

As is the earthy, such are they also that are earthy: and as is the heavenly, such are they also that are heavenly. 1 Corinthians 15:48

Those who are carnal operate in the flesh, but those who are spiritual operate in the Spirit.

Another beautiful scripture on this subject is this:

If ye then be risen with Christ, seek those things which are above, where Christ sitteth on the right hand of God. Colossians 3:1

This word *risen* means "resurrected." You cannot be resurrected if you have not first died to self. Resurrection can only take place if there is first a death. No wonder the Bible tells us to *"die daily."* Every time you die to the flesh you are partaking more and more of the resurrection. And there is power in the resurrection. Paul wrote:

A Call to Consecration

That I may know him, and the power of his resur-
rection, and the fellowship of his sufferings, being
made conformable unto his death; if by any means
I might attain unto the resurrection of the dead.
Philippians 3:10-11

"The fellowship of his sufferings" is overpowered by
"the power of his resurrection." If you are afraid to die,
cheer up. You have nothing to fear. There is coming
a resurrection unto life eternal.

Paul encouraged the Colossians:

If ye then be risen with Christ, seek those things
which are above, where Christ sitteth on the right
hand of God. Set your affection on things above,
not on things on the earth. For ye are dead, and
your life is hid with Christ in God. When Christ,
who is our life, shall appear, then shall ye also
appear with him in glory.   Colossians 3:1-4

What does a man who is earthy do? He seeks the
things of the earth. But a man who is of the Spirit
seeks the things that are of the Spirit. This is our
key. We are to *"set [our] affection on things above, not*
on things on the earth." Why? *"For ye are dead and your*

life is hid with Christ in God." That's powerful! Your life is preserved, protected, sheltered in Christ.

When Christ appears, we will also appear with Him in glory. That is your moment of glorification.

You cannot enter into glory unless you are first glorified. Why? Because flesh and blood cannot enter into the glory of God. In order for you to enter into the glory of God, you need to first of all be glorified, transformed, changed. The Bible tells us that God is changing us, transforming us, from glory to glory, from one level to another, from one height to another. Then, when He appears, we will appear with Him in glory.

These next verses are key:

> *Mortify therefore your members which are upon the earth; fornication, uncleanness, inordinate affection, evil concupiscence, and covetousness, which is idolatry: for which things' sake the wrath of God cometh on the children of disobedience: in the which ye also walked some time, when ye lived in them.*
>
> *But now ye also put off all these; anger, wrath, malice, blasphemy, filthy communication out of your mouth. Lie not one to another, seeing that*

A Call to Consecration

ye have put off the old man with his deeds; and have put on the new man, which is renewed in knowledge after the image of him that created him.

Colossians 3:5-10

What are the Scriptures telling us? First, that there is a better life, a glory, awaiting us. And, second, that we shall be united with Christ forever and never have to part from Him again. This is completion in God through Jesus Christ, our final destination, which is far greater than anything we have thus far seen, experienced, tasted, or felt in this life. That makes it worthwhile to remove anything and everything that might prevent us from gaining this glory.

We know that the wages of sin is death (see Romans 6:23) and that all have sinned and come short of the glory of God (see Romans 3:23). Sin will keep you from entering the glory of God, but I discovered something. Hebrews tells us: *"there remaineth ... a rest"* (Hebrews 4:9), one more rest, God's rest, in His presence, in His glory.

We have tasted a bit of Heaven down here and are experiencing a bit of God's glory as well. Sometimes we cannot handle it because our body doesn't know how to contain the glory and the power of the anointing of His presence. But what we have experienced is just a sprinkle of what is to come. There will be much more when He fully appears and we receive the fullness of His glory. In that moment, our bodies will be changed because this earthly body cannot contain the glory of God. It must be glorified. It must be transformed. It must be renewed because it cannot stand in the presence of God.

It was God who gave us new birth in Christ in the first place and it is God who will bring finish our maturity:

> *And the Lord make you to increase and abound in love one toward another, and toward all men, even as we do toward you: to the end he may stablish your hearts unblameable in holiness before God, even our Father, at the coming of our Lord Jesus Christ with all his saints.*
>
> 1 Thessalonians 3:12-13

Paul was referring to the Rapture of the Church, the coming of the Lord, and His catching away of His Bride. In the very next chapter, he teaches more about it:

A Call to Consecration

But I would not have you to be ignorant, brethren, concerning them which are asleep, that ye sorrow not, even as others which have no hope. For if we believe that Jesus died and rose again, even so them also which sleep in Jesus will God bring with him. For this we say unto you by the word of the Lord, that we which are alive and remain unto the coming of the Lord shall not prevent them which are asleep. For the Lord himself shall descend from heaven with a shout, with the voice of the archangel, and with the trump of God: and the dead in Christ shall rise first: then we which are alive and remain shall be caught up together with them in the clouds, to meet the Lord in the air: and so shall we ever be with the Lord. Wherefore comfort one another with these words. 1 Thessalonians 4:13-18

Paul began by speaking of those who have gone before us. It is always painful to lose someone you love. If that person was a Christian, it brings us some comfort. But if they were not, it causes us double sorrow, pain, and agony. As Paul stated here, we believe that Jesus died and rose again, and we therefore also believe that those who love and serve Him will also rise and experience eternal life.

Those who are dead without Christ have no hope, but those who are dead in Christ will be resurrected. They will come out of their graves and go with Jesus. And those of us who are alive at the coming of Christ will receive glorified bodies and rise to meet Him.

In that moment, that which was sown in weakness will be resurrected in power. That which was planted in corruption will be resurrected incorruptible. That which was sown mortal will be resurrected to immortality.

Get ready for that shout! Get ready for that declaration of the archangel! Get ready for that trumpet blast! It won't be long now! We have this hope. We have this blessed expectation, and therefore we are able to comfort each other.

Our sorrows, our trials, our tribulation are all momentary, but our life in glory will be forever. Jesus therefore said:

> *Let not your heart be troubled: ye believe in God, believe also in me. In my Father's house are many mansions: if it were not so, I would have told you. I go to prepare a place for you. And if I go and prepare a place for you, I will come again, and receive you unto myself; that where I am, there ye may be also.* John 14:1-3

A Call to Consecration

He was talking about the glory that is to come, about our translation, our glorification. These frail mortal bodies will be changed, glorified. Just as Jesus was planted in the grave in a corruptible body and then resurrected in a body that was no longer subject to the elements of time and space and could not be controlled, we shall be like Him when He shall appear. Like Him, our bodies will be glorified.

If you had a deaf ear, you will then hear perfectly. Your vision in your glorified body will be better than 20-20. You will have no more limitations and no flaws, for nothing will exist to corrupt you. You will be renewed like Jesus.

While we are waiting for that, there is an ordeal to traverse here on earth. Before a mother can enjoy the blessings of her child, she has to endure what is commonly called "labor pains." There is sometimes much suffering. But after the baby is born, she forgets the labor pains, the sorrow, the agony, the morning sickness, and life with that child brings her comfort, joy, and excitement. All of the agony and suffering are soon forgotten.

A cousin of mine, when giving birth to her first baby, nearly died. She went into a dry labor. She scratched at her husband and said, "This is all your fault," and declared, "No more!" Then, eleven months later, she was already three months pregnant again. They ended up having seven children. Every time the nurse would bring the new baby to her, she realized that all the pain, the sorrow, and the agony, were forgotten.

There's a greater glory awaiting us that cannot be compared to the sufferings, the trials, and the inconveniences of life in the here and now. We will come out of this trial completely perfect in Jesus Christ, purified as fine gold. We will emerge from this shell of a body and be like Jesus, as He is, in that glorified body, that glorified life. That is what He promised. He said He would present us before the Father spotless, blameless, and without wrinkle.

Paul's words are just as true today as when he wrote them:

> *The Spirit itself beareth witness with our spirit, that we are the children of God: and if children, then heirs; heirs of God, and joint-heirs with Christ; if so be that we suffer with him, that we may be also glorified together. For I reckon that the sufferings of this present time are not worthy to be*

*compared with the glory which shall be revealed
in us.*   Romans 8:16-18

Are you a child of God? Then you are destined for glorification. You are an heir of God and a joint-heir with Christ. You may have been called on to suffer with Him, but the promise is that you will be *"glorified together."*

Jesus wants us to be glorified even as He is glorified. We are His Body, and if the Head is glorified, the rest of the Body must be glorified.

It will happen, and when it does, the sufferings of the present time will be forgotten. Even if you are physically or financially bankrupt, whatever your physical situation is right now, know that the suffering of this present time is not worthy to be compared with the glory which shall be revealed in us.

The sufferings, the trials, the temptations that we are going through and struggling with right now cannot be compared to the glory which shall be revealed in us.

*For the earnest expectation of the creature waiteth
for the manifestation of the sons of God.*
                                   Romans 8:19

What does that mean? We are the sons of God, but we need to be manifested. Down here our manifestation is sometimes contrary to our confession of being children of God. As we continue through the process of sanctification, we will eventually come to the glorification.

> *For the creature was made subject to vanity, not willingly, but by reason of him who hath subjected the same in hope, because the creature itself also shall be delivered from the bondage of corruption into the glorious liberty of the children of God.*
>
> Romans 8:20-21

.

There is hope in God. Titus said it this way:

> *Looking for that blessed hope, and the glorious appearing of the great God and our Saviour Jesus Christ; who gave himself for us, that he might redeem us from all iniquity, and purify unto himself a peculiar people, zealous of good works.*
>
> Titus 2:13-14

That's the Rapture. That's our translation. That's the time when we will sing:

A Call to Consecration

Good-bye, old world, good-bye.
Don't you cry for me when I die.
Good-bye, old world, good-bye.

That song is older than I am, but it was a good one.
"Because the creature itself also shall be delivered from the bondage of corruption..." Who is the creature? You and I are the special creatures of God. We're not aliens. We are God's design. He said we would be *"delivered from the bondage of corruption into the glorious liberty of the children of God."* Hallelujah!

Then God said something strange:

> For we know that the whole creation groaneth
> and travaileth in pain together until now. And
> not only they, but ourselves also, which have the
> firstfruits of the Spirit, even we ourselves groan
> within ourselves, waiting for the adoption, to wit,
> the redemption of our body.   Romans 8:22-23

Your body is groaning. Why? Because you're hungry, you feel tired, you get exhausted, you get sleepy. In God, we go from blessing to blessing, but there are also some unpleasant experiences. It would have been wonderful if we had blessing all the time.

Sometimes when we land, it is difficult for us to take off again. We need a good Holy Ghost push.

In the meantime, we *"groan within ourselves waiting for the adoption, to wit, the redemption of our body."* This word *redemption* means there was a ransom to pay.

> *For we are saved by hope: but hope that is seen is not hope: for what a man seeth, why doth he yet hope for? But if we hope for that we see not, then do we with patience wait for it. Likewise the Spirit also helpeth our infirmities: for we know not what we should pray for as we ought: but the Spirit itself maketh intercession for us with groanings which cannot be uttered.* Romans 8:24-26

The Holy Spirit is at work inside of us to transform us. He is making intercession for us with groanings which cannot be uttered. He is searching our hearts and making intercession for the saints according to the will of God.

Now look at these last few verses.

> *Who shall separate us from the love of Christ? shall tribulation, or distress, or persecution, or famine, or nakedness, or peril, or sword? As it is*

written, For thy sake we are killed all the day long; we are accounted as sheep for the slaughter. Nay, in all these things we are more than conquerors through him that loved us. For I am persuaded, that neither death, nor life, nor angels, nor principalities, nor powers, nor things present, nor things to come, nor height, nor depth, nor any other creature, shall be able to separate us from the love of God, which is in Christ Jesus our Lord.

Romans 8:35-39

That should excite you. Now let's look at the prophet Haggai:

Who is left among you that saw this house in her first glory? and how do ye see it now? is it not in your eyes in comparison of it as nothing?   Haggai 2:3

He was speaking of the Temple in Jerusalem. Only the elderly could remember it in its greatest glory. What did it look like now? The comparison was *"as nothing."*

How about your body? Do you suffer from arthritis, migraine headaches, or some other physical malady? Don't you wish you could bring back the days of your youth?

The thought continues in verse 5:

According to the word that I covenanted with you when ye came out of Egypt, so my spirit remaineth among you: fear ye not. For thus saith the LORD of hosts; Yet once, it is a little while, and I will shake the heavens, and the earth, and the sea, and the dry land; and I will shake all nations, and the desire of all nations shall come: and I will fill this house with glory, saith the LORD of hosts

.   Haggai 2:5-7

The prophet Haggai was talking about the Temple, but we're talking about your body, your earthly house. It may very well not be nearly as glorious as it once was. But Haggai continued:

The glory of this latter house shall be greater than of the former, saith the LORD of hosts: and in this place will I give peace, saith the LORD of hosts.   Haggai 2:9

The glory of the latter house will be greater than the former. The latter house, your glorified body, will no longer be subject to time and space and earthly corruptions. You will be able to time travel like a spirit, like the wind. A wall will not be able to prevent your passage. A grave will not be able to hold you down. You will walk through closed doors and pass through walls. Why? Because you have been glorified. Your current beauty cannot be compared with the beauty that is awaiting you.

Your looks now are nothing compared to what you will be when you are glorified. Women, you are beautiful now. Men, you are good looking now. But Just wait until you become like Christ in a glorified body.

When Jesus shall appear, you shall be like Him. I love that song:

What a day that will be
When my Jesus I shall see.
And I look upon His face,
The one who saved me by His grace.
When He takes me by the hand,
And leads me through the Promised Land.
What a day, glorious day, that will be.[2]

---

2. Songwriter: Jim Hill. Lyrics © Ben Speer Music

Are you looking forward to that day? Are you anticipating His arrival? Then, mortify your body. Be sanctified! Be cleansed! Be holy! Eternal life is waiting for you.

Tell the Lord today:

Lord, give me grace.
Give me endurance.
Help me, Lord God,
to look beyond this life
into that life that is waiting for me.

The glory we are currently experiencing is nothing compared to the glory and the fullness of what is to come. We shall be changed in a moment in a twinkling of an eye, and we shall be like Him.

Today you can say to the devil, "No matter what you do, no matter how much you try, you will not succeed. I have a life, a glorious life, awaiting me, and I am determined to press through every trouble necessary to get there."

There is a beautiful testimony that Job left us:

A Call to Consecration

And though after my skin worms destroy this body, yet in my flesh shall I see God. Job 19:26

Cheer up, beloved. Greater days are ahead of us. Jesus is coming again, and He's coming very soon. When He appears, we shall be changed. We shall be caught up to meet Him in the air. We won't need to buy an airline ticket. And this time we won't be limited to fly at 30,000 to 40,000 feet, as modern airliners are. We will zoom past all the galaxies and enter into the portals of Heaven.

You won't need to be worried about turbulence or the hours it takes to fly long distances. In the wink of an eye, you'll be there.

Control your body. Let it groan if it needs to be groaning, but let it groan for the glory. Let it groan toward Heaven. Let it groan toward the life that Christ has for us.

Thank You, Lord. We shall be glorified. He is coming soon. Praise the Lord! Amen!

This, beloved, is a call to consecration.

AUTHOR CONTACT PAGE

You may contact Bishop Ray Llarena directly at:

Global Evangelistic Ministries
9039 Lakeshore Dr.
Pleasant Prairie, WI 53158

Email: bishopray1@yahoo.com

www.ingramcontent.com/pod-product-compliance
Lightning Source LLC
Chambersburg PA
CBHW030937090426
42737CB00007B/464